Testimonials

"Please know that you are not reading this book by accident! I believe it is by divine appointment from the Lord that you are learning more about His workings through this book, *Across Alabama,* and how He uses his servant, Paul Schweigert, in accomplishing His purposes. I've walked with Paul many times carrying the cross, and have seen how God will meet each and every person wherever they are in their lives. I pray that the Lord ministers to you and stirs mightily in your heart as you read these stories."

Steve Hines
Businessman, and frequent walking companion with Paul
Birmingham, Alabama

"Christianity is more than a religion—it is about relationships. *Across Alabama* is a story of how Paul Schweigert pours his relationship with God into many other people across Alabama. You will never read another book like this one, which offers a real answer to our ultimate need for a relationship with God."

Raymond F. Culpepper, D.D.
Church of God International Offices
Cleveland, Tennessee

"In reading *Across Alabama*, you will encounter all types of people, including country folk, high-ranking governmental officials, individuals of all races, caring and generous individuals, and individuals who have been deceived by evil. You will read about people who live in the same state but seem to live in completely different worlds. Regardless of their differences, however, they have one thing in common: God loves them all. *Across Alabama* contains an inspiring journey that ends with a map as to how you can find God's love, along with the peace and purpose that it brings."

Douglas B. Kauffman
Attorney
Birmingham, Alabama

"*Across Alabama* illustrates the powerful message of the gospel, and readers will be encouraged and challenged by the dynamic stories and the continual faithfulness of God in the midst of a lost world."

David Wray II
Graduate student, and frequent walking companion with Paul
Birmingham, Alabama

ACROSS ALABAMA

Meeting People and Trusting God

Paul Schweigert

Library of Congress Catalog Card Number:
2007926481

ISBN: 978-1-59684-279-3
© Copyright 2007 by Paul Schweigert
All Rights Reserved
Printed by *Derek Press*, Cleveland, TN

The author may be contacted as follows:
Paul Schweigert
P.O. Box 26211
Birmingham, AL 35260-0211

Many names have been changed to protect the privacy
of the individuals involved.

Order This Book

100% of the proceeds from the sale of this book
will be reinvested in the creation, translation and publication
of materials for spiritual seekers in Alabama
and around the world.

You may secure a copy of this book by contacting
any one of the following:

1) The publisher: Derek Press
1080 Montgomery Ave. NE
Cleveland, TN 37311
Call 1-800-553-8506 to place order, or order online at
www.pathwaybookstore.com by typing in the name of the book.

2) Your favorite bookstore:
This book may be ordered from your favorite bookstore
by giving the following information:
Name of book:
Across Alabama: Meeting People and Trusting God
Publisher: *Derek Press*
Publisher's phone number: 1-800-553-8506
Publisher's Web site: *www.pathwaybookstore.com*
Author: Paul Schweigert

3) Order online also at *Amazon.com*

Dedication

To my sweet and beautiful wife, whose mature walk with the Lord and sensitive spirit have provided me a spiritual sounding board and companion in ministry to the many people of Alabama.

With all my love, I dedicate this book to:
Connie S. Schweigert

Table of Contents

Foreword

Abrave missionary by the name of Jim Elliott once prayed, "Oh, that God would make us dangerous. . . ." Jim's prayer was the honest confession of a guy who refused to live within the safe confines of "conventional Christianity." Jim longed to live life "on the edge" in the passionate pursuit of the redemptive plan and purpose of God for this planet. He did.

Paul Schweigert is a "dangerous" man. He's dangerous because he is courageous enough to take God at His word and believe that God cares about people regardless of their background, ethnicity, or past. He's dangerous because he believes we need to "pull out all stops" in an effort to share the message of God's extravagant love as revealed in the cross of Jesus Christ.

Are you tired of just going through the motions? Do you long for a life of adventure, freedom and significance? Check out the "dangerous" message in this book. It could change your life.

Chris Goins, Senior Pastor
Metropolitan Church of God
Birmingham, Alabama

Acknowledgments

It's very difficult to write a book without the help of other people. I am very thankful to everyone who has assisted me in any way during this four-year process. Furthermore, I offer special recognition to the following individuals who have made substantial contributions:

Thank you, Doug Kauffman, Jonathan Schweigert, Christy Schweigert, and Connie Schweigert, for reading countless early drafts and making helpful suggestions that kept me pointed in the right direction. You should be given a trophy for your patience. As I look back, I understand just how bad those early drafts were.

Thank you, Bruce Akin and Dr. Floyd Carey, for your publishing suggestions. You helped me better understand my strengths and weaknesses as I headed into the publication process.

Thank you, Ashley McCleery, for your help in the early editing of this book.

Thank you, Jessie Sirbaugh, for serving as my copy editor, and for all your help in guiding me through the final stages of this book.

Thank you, Pat Whary and Jerry Puckett, and your staff at Derek Press, for all your hard work and patience with me in making this publication become a reality. Thank you, R. Ariel

Vázquez, for your contributions in connection with the front cover and the formatting of this book.

Thank you, John and Sherrie Crawford, Steve and Leigh Ann Hines, Dwight and Amy Elliott, Frank and Susan Clay, Del and Rose Nicholson, Al and Pattie Yother, David and Shelia Wray, David and Kim Dixon, Mike and Gina Kerby, Cary and Amy Miller, Fred and Reneea Ross, Ivan and Lydia Griffin, and many other friends and relatives, for your faithful prayers and help concerning this project.

Introduction

I'm an Alabama boy who loves most everything about my state. I love the passion for college sports, the great local barbecue, the northeastern hills, the fertile Black Belt, and the white beaches on the Gulf Coast. But most of all, I have fallen in love with the people of my state. This heart-of-the-South region, still maturing from the harsh civil rights struggle a generation ago, is filled with people of dissimilar culture, economic status, and beliefs. The more diverse the local population, the more intriguing I've found their tales.

For many of my adult years I was an upper-class businessman and had no desire to be otherwise. More than two decades passed before the Lord spoke to my heart about a spiritual undertaking. I now walk the streets, roads and highways of Alabama bearing a spiritual symbol: a cross. Along with this calling, the Lord has given me compassion for those individuals who are earnestly searching for meaning and purpose in their life.

I started walking full-time with the cross on December 6, 1995. My normal walking routine each day is as follows:

1. I drive to the Alabama county the Lord has currently placed upon my heart.

2. After parking at the turnaround point I reached the previous day, I unbolt my cross from the truck.

3. Placing the cross on my shoulder, I walk along a highway or within a neighborhood for several hours.

As I walk I pass people in their cars, their yards, in town, or at their workplace. They often stop in their vehicles to ask questions. Many times people ask, "What do you hope to accomplish by walking around my community with that cross?" I actually ask the Lord a similar question about what He wants me to accomplish in each new area I walk. As He speaks to my heart, I try to obey.

Pictured is my 2002 Ford truck with my 12-foot cross extending out the back. My last two trucks were a 1993 Dodge Dakota and a 1976 GMC.

Now when I look back through my journals documenting the first years of the cross walk, I am amazed at my walking schedule of 6-10 miles almost every weekday. I was so focused on what the Lord called me to do that I woke up each morning driven spiritually and emotionally to get started again. After eight months of continuous walking, my knees, calves and feet became bruised a solid purple due to the weight of the cross and the constant pounding of my feet on city streets. My shoulders were constantly cut and bruised by the cross.

Here I am unloading the cross from the specially built truck bed frame.

During these exciting but tiring days, the Lord gave me the following specific objectives:

1. Be a *visual witness* for Christ with the cross.
2. Be a *verbal witness* for Christ to spiritual seekers.
3. Be a *discipleship leader* through Bible studies.
4. Be an *encourager* to the saints.

Writing this book is not an attempt to detail everything the Lord did, but rather to document only what God absolutely stirs in my heart to tell. I relied heavily on 1,500 pages of journal notes to write these chapters. I have previously told of the events that occurred during the first six months of the cross walk, including the personal crisis that led to the start of this journey, in the book *Why I Walk With a Cross.*

The chronicle that follows relates happenings from August, 1996, to the end of 1999. Join me now as I share stories from the next 10 counties to which the Lord called me. As you read these pages, you are guaranteed to meet some very interesting people. May God give you a happy heart and an open mind as you follow my trail through Alabama.

Here I am talking with retired schoolteacher Doug Borden. I walk from town to town talking with people as I walk. Then, I usually spend several weeks walking and ministering in each town when I arrive. I still drive home to Connie each evening.

Part 1

WHERE IS THIS JESUS CROSS TAKING ME?

Chapter One

ENCOUNTER
WITH THE
HATE GROUP

While driving through a tiny community in north Alabama late one afternoon, I was shocked to see four hooded figures standing shoulder to shoulder at the main intersection with their right arms extended upward and outward in a Third Reich salute. The men were wearing white gowns made of something similar to bedsheet material with hoods that draped over their heads and faces. The hoods were fashioned in the shape of a cone, with the tip of the cone above their heads. The only visible parts of each person's flesh were their hands, which hung beyond the arms of their gowns, and their eyes, which peered through two small slits in their hoods.

Turning in disbelief to speak with my wife who was riding in the van beside me, I was interrupted by my two young daughters' shrieks and questions. When I mentioned the words "hate group," the girls quickly ducked their heads beneath the back-seat covers. Turning again to my wife, I said, "Connie, I can't believe this foolishness!"

By now I was looking at the hoodsmen in my rearview mirror. "I walked this very spot with my Jesus cross less than two months ago, and I resent their presence here. This is making a mockery of the cross! I'm turning around—I need to speak with these guys." And with that comment, I slowed my vehicle and wheeled around.

As I parked my vehicle beside the white-clad demonstrators, I could feel my blood pressure rising. I gave instructions to my wife to drive off without me if trouble started. Connie started praying as I locked the van doors, and she looked back with uneasiness toward the girls.

Our day had started out simple enough. We had traveled over 100 miles from our home to visit friends in north Alabama, and we were now headed to a second destination to see other friends. Earlier I had walked many miles in this same community with my 12-foot wooden Jesus cross, telling locals about the love of Jesus who died on the cross. But love was not the feeling I had right now—I was aggravated and upset.

I introduced myself to the four hooded men and quickly asked, "Who are you, and what are you doing here?" They dropped their salutes as they faced me. Two of the men introduced themselves by giving their first names.

One man stated, "We're telling people today what a great unit we have here."

"How can you use the word *great*? Your agenda is to bring misery to the lives of people you hate!"

"No it ain't—our agenda is law and order."

"Law and order for whom? For yourselves?"

"Naw, for the people of our community."

"I doubt the people of this community want your kind of law and order," I insisted.

"Oh yeah they do! We have many fine citizens in our group. Men who are highly respected around these here parts."

More vehicles drove past us, and the four men waved at the occupants. Some of the passengers waved back.

"These men you say who are highly respected—what are they highly respected for?" I asked.

"For keeping law and order in our community," two voices exclaimed in unison.

"I don't suppose the law and order you keep speaking of has anything to do with people who are different than you—people who look, live and speak a little different?"

The one who appeared to be the leader answered, "Listen here fellow, we're trying to keep the family values the same as they've always been around here for generations. We don't like change. We want the same kind of people living here who have always lived here. You know what I mean. We want things to stay the same. We have good people in our group. You should meet some of them!"

"I'm really not interested in meeting your so-called good men. Actually, I've already met several people in this community. I walked this very road several weeks ago with my Jesus cross."

"Oh, you're the man," another hooded figure spoke out quickly. "We really like the cross!"

"Don't say that—I greatly resent that! *You all* misrepresent the cross. The cross is not about hate, but love. How can you like the cross but still continue to hate?"

Staying calm was becoming increasingly difficult. I was also not aware of the irony of my own words. I was speaking of love, yet my tone of voice, my body language, and my feelings were expressing anything but love.

"We here fellows like the cross, but we hate change," another countered.

We talked for a while longer, but I could tell I was getting nowhere. We were just talking in circles.

"I have to go," I stated. "I just want you to understand that I disagree with everything you stand for, and I resent your use and misrepresentation of the cross!" With that, I started walking back toward my van. I looked up to see two big sets of young eyes staring at us over the dashboard of my van, which was still running.

"Hold on, man," the leader shouted out. "Not so fast." He quickly stepped beside me. "You have no understanding of the good things we do around here and the great men we have in our organization. For example, a man named Josh—I want you to meet him yourself. He's a great man. Come to our rally in the woods tonight to see for yourself!" He pointed with his thumb over and behind his head.

"No way!" I said. "I'm meeting some friends for a Bible study in a few minutes. That secret meeting of yours is no place for me." As I walked to my van, my wife unlocked the door. I drove off, shaking my head in disgust. Connie let out a sigh of relief. We sat in quiet reprieve for the next few moments as I drove down the road.

Chapter Two

DECISION TIME

The Invitation

L eaving the scene of the four hooded men, I drove my family to our friends' home 30 miles away. Connie and I discussed these men and the conversation that had just taken place. Our dialogue was interspersed with quietness as I replayed the events in my mind. During the silence, the still small voice of the Lord spoke to me. The voice wasn't audible. Nevertheless, I heard it just the same. "Paul, you were invited to the rally in the woods tonight. You should go! These men may appear different to you, but My story is the same."

My first reaction was, *Oh no, the Lord wouldn't expect me to go to a hate-group meeting. How ridiculous!* But the more I thought about the invitation, the more I realized God was indeed speaking to my heart about taking a stand for Jesus at the rally. By this time I had been walking with the cross full-time in Alabama for nine months, but nothing in my experiences had prepared me for this situation. I had walked in many other tough places in

Alabama. But this invitation was for an event at night, in a remote wooded area, and involved men with whom I disagreed.

As I talked with Connie, I mentioned the invitation. She saw me squirming as I wrestled within. Finally, I acknowledged that I felt the Lord was leading me to their meeting that night. I asked for her help in preparing my thoughts for the evening. By this time we had reached our destination.

Inside our friends' home, I explained the encounter to six other adults. I then asked for their help also in preparation for my reunion with the four hooded men and their unit. Much conversation ensued.

One man at the Bible study told of a recent event that had taken place not many miles from his own house. A minority family moved into a house in a nearby neighborhood only to find a cross burning in their front yard the first evening. This gesture was intended to inflict fear and a warning of events to come. The next morning, the family loaded up their belongings and vacated the area. This story confirmed to me the probable intentions of this hate group.

I needed appropriate scriptures if I was to speak to this group. So Connie and I, along with our friends, spent precious time together finding scriptures we hoped would be applicable. We discussed many possibilities, and I wrote inside the front cover of my paperback New Testament several verses that spoke to my heart. Finally, I decided that once I was there I'd let the Holy Spirit lead me in exactly what to say.

My wife and friends agreed to partner with me in prayer while I went on to the meeting. We also prayed together fervently before I left. I kissed Connie goodbye, hoping it would not be the last. She had been through so much change since the cross walk started that I felt badly about putting her through another terrible worry. But I also knew that when the going got rough, she knew how to channel her concerns into powerful prayer.

Now that I had decided to go, knowing exactly where to go loomed as a major obstacle. The only directions I had were the image of a man's thumb pointing down a lonely road into a heavily wooded area. It was now well after dark, and the evening was filled with many unknowns.

My Search for the Rally Site

Driving back to the small community intersection where all this started, I turned onto the rural road the man pointed to earlier. Several miles passed before I saw any sign of life. Finally, I found a volunteer fire department with its large bay doors open and a dozen firemen and friends playing cards on tables in front of the fire trucks.

"Does anyone know the location of the rally tonight?" I asked.

"I do," one man answered matter-of-factly. "I'll show you the location here on this wall map."

He gave me exact instructions in the general direction from which I had just come. I thanked him and walked back to my van. On second thought, I turned around and returned to the card tables.

"By the way, my name is Paul. I asked you for directions to the rally tonight not because I agree with this group's philosophy, but because I want to share Jesus Christ. My desire is to give a contrary opinion at the rally tonight. I also hope that *you* do not fall for the fear preached by this hate group."

Everyone just stared at me and then at each other. Two women opened their mouths like they wanted to say something, but nothing came out.

A tall, stocky man stepped forward and asked, "Who is going with you to the rally tonight? How many people?"

"Just myself," I replied.

He motioned for me to follow him back to my van. He asked me the same questions again, and I gave him the same answers. Then he stated, "Sir . . . all I can say is . . . be careful! Just be very, very careful!"

The big man then shifted his weight from side to side and ran his hands through his hair, looking worried. Driving back down the road, I thought to myself, *I sure hope I heard correctly from the Lord about being here tonight!*

Chapter Three

THE RALLY

After receiving directions from the fireman, I found the hate-group rally down a narrow county road. I saw the flicker of flashlights before barely making out the turnoff spot. The night was overcast and pitch-dark, without the glow of moon or stars. The presence of evil hung over the place like a cloud.

As I turned off the road, I noticed an old reel-to-reel movie camera mounted on a tripod at the entrance. I flicked my headlights onto high beam. The rally site was a large hay field surrounded on all sides by a heavy tree line. A man in white garb walked up to my van window. His hood was replaced by a telephone headset. I introduced myself and stated that four men out on the highway had invited me. I further stated that I had come to talk about Jesus and to voice a contrary opinion.

"Oh yes, I remember you," the man with the headset responded. "I was one of those men who talked with you this afternoon."

After additional conversation, he spoke into the headset with someone who was located in another area of the field. He then instructed me to park my van about 100 yards across the field against the trees. Once parked, I opened my door and spoke to two hooded men who had been peering into my side window.

"I live in the Birmingham area, and I was invited this afternoon to come to your rally. I would like permission to speak to your group."

"We can't give you permission to do nothing, but we'll take you to somebody else." With that comment, they instructed me to follow them.

I was presented to several groups of men. Each group struggled as to how to respond to my request about speaking to their entire assembly. Their eyes peered out at me from narrow openings. They occasionally gave me their first names but never their last names or any other information. I tried to respond in the opposite manner—giving my full name, my telephone number, and the general area where I lived in Birmingham. I had nothing to hide. However, many of them appeared very jittery.

As we walked deeper into the field, my eyes gradually adjusted to the dark. At the far end of the large meadow was a spotlight beaming its light toward a podium. The indirect illumination from the spotlight now provided enough light to easily distinguish the white flowing figures around me.

At last, I was presented to the grand leader of this local unit, and about 20 men surrounded me. Two guards were placed behind me while the remainder of the men stood in a semicircle in front of me. We were now located in the middle of the large, enclosed field. I again presented my request to speak from the podium located farther up the field.

"Why do you want to speak to us?" the leader inquired.

"I talk to people all over Alabama about Jesus, and I want to speak to this group also."

"Yes, but what would you speak about?"

"I have a little Bible here, and I would read some verses and talk about the Lord."

"OK, but what would you say after reading those words?"

"Again, I would just talk about the Lord, sir. I'm not here to cut you down or to talk in a degrading way toward your group." Fortunately, the Lord gave me an attitude adjustment earlier in the evening or my answer might have been different. Plus, I was substantially outnumbered!

The leader continued to ask me question after question, wanting to know exactly what I would say to the group. It finally dawned on me that he was afraid I would offend the group by what I said. *What a paradox*, I thought, *a hate group worried about being offended!* Finally, I told the leader I would not make any comment or commentary of my own if he would only let me speak at the podium. I would just read Scripture.

"If you read from that Bible, what kind of verses would you read?" the leader questioned.

"Well, how about these two scripture verses for starters? This first one is from my cross walk theme verse: 'For it is time to seek the Lord' (Hosea 10:12). The second scripture is from the New Testament: '"Teacher, which is the greatest commandment in the Law?" Jesus replied: "'Love the Lord your God with all your heart and with all your soul and with all your mind.' This is the first and greatest commandment. And the second is like it: 'Love your neighbor as yourself'"' (Matthew 22:36-39)."

After reading the words, "Love your neighbor as yourself," many of the white hoods starting shaking from side to side, and several men responded at once with their leader, "We *do not* like those kinds of verses!"

I countered, "Men, if what you are doing and thinking lines up with the Word of God, you will welcome these verses I want to read. However, if what's in your heart is contrary to the Word of God, then some of these verses may make you feel uncomfortable."

There was much commotion at this point as everyone was talking at the same time. The leader walked up to me and said he wanted me to meet a man named Josh, and with that statement he walked away. Two guards escorted me to the side and, after a few minutes, I was introduced to Josh.

Chapter Four

THE RALLY
CONCLUSION

Meeting Josh

After being introduced to Josh, I once again explained who I was. I also told Josh that I wanted permission to speak to the group about Jesus from the podium located up the field.

"Oh no. You need to let *me* speak to these men about the Lord," Josh countered. "After all, I'm the chaplain around here."

"You're what?"

"I'm the chaplain."

"You're the chaplain where?"

Josh was standing there with only his eyeballs visible to me as I tried to read his thoughts. I just couldn't comprehend a chaplain participating in this setting, and my disbelief was obvious.

"I'm telling you—I'm the chaplain for these men! I talk to them about spiritual things sometimes. A few of them will listen

. . . sometimes."

"It's just dawned on me, Josh, that you're the man those four guys on the highway talked about this afternoon. They said I needed to meet you. They even called you a great man. Why are you great? Who are you Josh?"

"Well, I'm not sure I'm great, but I'll tell you who I am. I come to these meetings here on Saturday night, and then I preach in many of the local churches around here on Sunday morning."

I was stunned! I couldn't speak! I could hardly move! I stood there like a stump for minutes without making a sound. In spite of having lived my entire life in Alabama, I was totally unprepared for what I had just heard. I was heartsick—I just couldn't comprehend the evil I had just heard.

About this time the rally started up the field, and it was extremely loud. A man stood at the podium and yelled out one line into the microphone, and then the crowd responded.

"Are we gonna lose control in our communities?"

"White suprem . . . acy!" the crowd responded.

"Are we gonna sit back and do nothing?"

"White suprem . . . acy!"

"Are we gonna establish law and order?"

"White suprem . . . acy!"

"Do we have the answers for today?"

"White suprem . . . acy!"

"What is the answer for today?"

"White suprem . . . acy!"

The rest of what I heard I do not care to recount. That crowd of hooded members was quickly stirring itself into a frenzy. I turned back to Josh and tried to reason with him from Scripture. I talked to him in a slow, calm manner. However, we found very little common ground between us. Sometimes, Josh tried to understand what I was saying, but he just couldn't grab hold of it with any real faith.

"Josh, do you believe we can pray and trust God to provide food and shelter for our families?"

"Sure, man."

"Do you believe we can pray and trust God to heal our children when they are sick?"

"Why, sure!"

"Then why can't we trust God, and Him alone, to solve our community problems? Why do we have to take matters into our own hands?"

"If we don't take matters into our own hands, we will lose control."

"But isn't that the idea—to lose control by turning the control over to God? How about these verses:

> 'Have faith in God,' Jesus answered. 'I tell you the truth, If anyone says to this mountain, "Go, throw yourself into the sea," and does not doubt in his heart but believes that what he says will happen, it will be done for him. Therefore I tell you, whatever you ask for in prayer, believe that you have received it, and it will be yours. And when you stand praying, if you hold anything against anyone, forgive him, so that your Father in heaven may forgive you your sins' (Mark 11:22-25).

"Josh, why won't these verses work in our communities?"

"There are some things you must do yourself."

"But, Josh, why not fall on your face for a year and ask God to either take care of things in your community or take care of you—to either change your community or change you? Why not try having faith in God?"

"All that reasoning sounds good when you say it that way, Paul. But all I know is we can't lose control!"

After Josh and I finished our discussion, a member of the group whispered something in Josh's ear. Josh then informed me that I would not be permitted to speak at the podium. We said goodbye to each other, and I was escorted to my van. An old patrol car with the lights turned off tailed me to the dark exit.

Lessons Learned

I was very disappointed that I wasn't permitted to speak at the hate rally. However, it occurred to me later that I had spoken to over half the men at the rally in my unsuccessful attempts to speak at the podium. So, really, I had accomplished my mission—placing the name of Jesus front and center before many of these men.

During the late-night drive home from the hate rally, I asked the Lord, "What cross walk lessons am I to learn from all that happened tonight?" The Lord began to speak to my heart the following spiritual lessons. As I wrote these lessons down in my Bible in the early hours of the morning, I had no idea what experiences lay ahead, or how often I would refer to, or relearn, these same lessons.

1. *Beware* of influential men in high places (even in the church) who seek to bring credibility to an evil cause. (I thought of Judas, one of the disciples, in the arrest of Jesus, as described in Matthew 26:14-16.)

2. Be willing to use *Biblical truth* to confront falsehood. (I remembered 2 Timothy 2:15.)

3. *Reliance on God* (through prayer), instead of self-reliance, is a much more effective way to solve tough community issues or any other issues. (I thought of the entire book of Nehemiah for many examples.)

4. *Love* is a greater power than prejudice. (I often read 1 Corinthians 13, which is also known as "The Love Chapter.")

5. *Courage* is from the Lord, but fear is from the devil. (I remembered Ephesians 6:10-18, which reads in part, "Finally, be strong in the Lord and in his mighty power. Put on the full armor of God so that you can take your stand against the devil's schemes.")

The Hate Rally Aftermath

Immediately after leaving the hate rally and before my drive home, my body shook as I sat in the parking lot of a convenience store. By this time I was miles down the road from the rally and still trying to deal with the evening's events. A question had just entered my mind. This was not a thought of fear, but more one of bewilderment and amazement: *Where in the world is this Jesus cross taking me?*

I had enjoyed safe office jobs all my life until less than a year ago. Now I was walking outdoors in all kinds of weather carrying a 12-foot wooden cross and talking about Jesus in settings that I could never have envisioned.

A month before, I walked for 30 days around Birmingham's Legion Field in connection with the 1996 Olympic Soccer Games. I experienced massive crowds around this converted football field as Birmingham played host to soccer teams from around the world, including the U.S. Olympic team.

In the months before this hate-group rally and the Olympic Games, I walked mainly in the Greater-Birmingham and Greater-Huntsville areas. Now I longed to get out in the country and away from the traffic for a while. But I could see that the Alabama countryside had its own unique challenges I'd have to deal with. The realization of what could be ahead shook me to the core!

Where is this Jesus cross taking me?

Part 2

WALKING ALABAMA COUNTY BY COUNTY

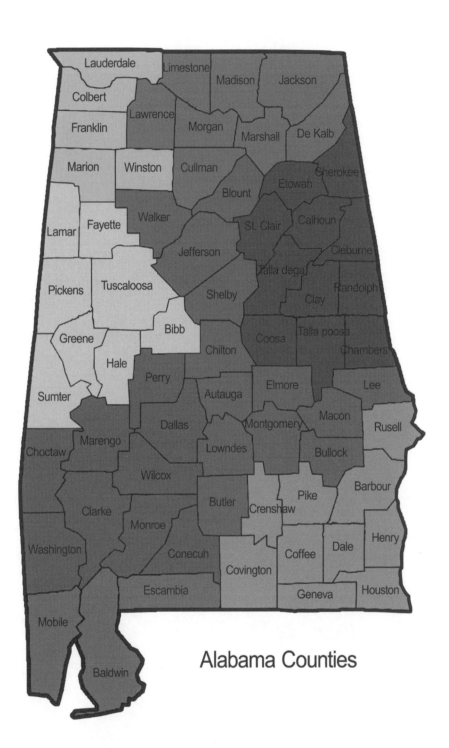

Alabama Counties

Chapter Five

LIGHTNING

Introduction

I knew God had called me to walk in Alabama one county at a time, but the job at this point seemed overwhelming. I couldn't comprehend spending a long time in just one county when north and central Alabama alone had 40 counties. I spent only six weeks in Etowah County, but I should have spent many months. I'm sure now that I didn't allow enough time for relationships to develop properly in this county of over 100,000 residents. However, I did meet a lot of people, and several Bible studies were started.

The city of Gadsden, a blue-collar working town, dominates every facet of this county. I spent most of my time walking in Greater-Gadsden, but I also walked the highways in the rural areas of Etowah County.

Shoes or No Shoes

Although the number of days I walked there were few, the days I did walk in Etowah County were long and hard. While in this county, I purchased my fourth pair of tennis shoes since the cross walk started. The third pair of shoes had lasted me 600 miles, which was 300 miles too many. Actually, I remember my third pair of shoes very clearly. At the 400-mile mark, I put cardboard inside the shoes because the toes and heels were wearing through. I was already wearing two pairs of socks to cut down on the blisters. At the 600-mile point, there was more cardboard than shoe on my feet. Still, God's hand was on my back each morning, pushing me out the door.

My feet hurt terribly on the first day I wore the new pair of tennis shoes that replaced my "Old Faithfuls." I guess my feet rejected change. On the third day, the skin on my right heel peeled completely off. But, as always, there was an urgency to keep walking and talking. The following day I walked through downtown Gadsden with my bedroom slipper taped onto my right foot because it felt more comfortable than my new tennis shoes.

But don't feel sorry for me because I was happy as a lark, doing what God had called me to do. Besides, a scarcity of funds in those early years was nothing new. But my point here is that the Spirit of God was stirring in me to walk and talk, and I was doing everything I could to be obedient.

Visual Image of the Cross

I'm often encouraged by how God uses just the visual image of the cross to work in people's hearts. I heard the following comments on the streets of Etowah County by individuals who saw the cross:

- A lady told me, "Two days before you walked by our house with the cross, I prayed that God would send someone to us with the gospel." When this lady saw the cross, she knew that was her answer to prayer. For the next year, I taught a Bible study in her home with her family members and friends.
- A lady said, "I was fired from my job last week. The day I was fired I was driving home and thinking, *This job loss is my cross to bear.* I looked up, and there you were with Jesus' cross! I was greatly encouraged."
- A man named Kenneth stated, "I saw you walking with the cross several days ago. I went home and told my wife what I had seen and that we needed to get back in church again!"
- A 29-year-old man stopped to say, "My wife died just two weeks ago. I really needed to see the cross today!"

Lightning Lesson

I was walking one afternoon in a small town south of Gadsden. It began to rain extremely hard, and then a lightning storm set in. The lightning flashed every few seconds literally right above my head. I could find nowhere safe to hide. Before I realized what was ahead of me, I was walking across a long bridge over a body of water.

The water on my side of the bridge was so deep it easily covered my tennis shoes and ankles. The cross resting on my shoulder was the highest object on the bridge, and I knew that was not a good situation in an electrical storm. The lightning was blinding me. In desperation I cried out loud, "Lord, please stop the lightning, in Jesus' name!"

The lightning stopped instantly and completely, but the rain continued even harder. I finally made it back to my vehicle about a mile away. A block from my truck, I thought, *I wonder if God really heard my prayer, or would the lightning have stopped regardless?*

No sooner had that thought passed through my mind than a powerful lightning strike hit nearby, and the thunder shook the ground around me like an earthquake. I immediately raised my hands toward heaven and said, "Thank you, Jesus, for hearing my prayer!"

This was an early lesson about trusting God, and it would serve me well many times in the future as I trusted God for impossible situations. By the way, the name of the town where God heard and answered my lightning prayer was *Rainbow City*!

Chapter Six

A HAUNTING CONVERSATION

DeKalb County:
October 1996 to December 1996

Alabama the Beautiful

O f all the places I've walked in Alabama, DeKalb County has to be one of the most beautiful and romantic. Desoto Falls, which is located near Mentone, is one of my favorite spots in all of Alabama because of its sheer beauty. I imagine many young couples have experienced their first kiss at this breathtaking spot. I've sure enjoyed taking my pretty wife, Connie, there on many occasions.

Little River Canyon is another memorable place in DeKalb County. You can drive for miles along the rim of this majestic canyon with the Little River flowing hundreds of feet below. The scenery there in autumn is unforgettable.

DeKalb County has more dirt roads than almost any other county in Alabama. Some of these roads offer visages from a century ago. Unfortunately, I had to drive 200-250 round-trip miles a day to reach this land of beauty. But I had the great privilege of walking through small towns and on remote dirt roads as the colors were changing in this rustic, idyllic county. I also talked with hundreds of wonderful people. However, one conversation eclipsed all my other memories of DeKalb County.

DeSoto Falls in DeKalb County is one of my favorite sights in Alabama.

Little River Canyon, with its deep gorges, extends for miles in northeast Alabama.

Here I am walking in front of the White Hall Methodist Church.

Here I am enjoying a warm autumn day in Dekalb County.

A Man Named Arnold

I was walking in a little community one day when a man named Arnold stopped in his automobile to talk. After chatting for a while, I asked Arnold if he knew the Lord.

Arnold replied, "I've been going to such and such church down the road since I was a young boy, and I've hardly missed a Sunday my whole life."

Our conversation then continued in other directions. After a few minutes, I asked Arnold the question a second time, "Arnold, do you know the Lord?"

This man, age 65 or so, looked at me in surprise.

"Look, not only have I gone to church all my life, but I've raised my children in the same church. I now sit with all my grandchildren every Sunday in that same church."

I was very impressed with this grandfather's faithfulness to church, and I congratulated him for his good example to his family. Once again our conversation moved on to other things. But I felt a tug in my heart. When the right time came, I ventured again with a gentle voice, "Arnold, you still have not directly answered my question—do you know Jesus as your personal Lord and Savior?"

Arnold's reply disturbed me as he spoke. "No, I don't know Jesus! I've sat in that same church all my life, but I've never accepted Jesus into my heart. I know that if I were to die today, I would go straight to hell."

I now understood why this gentleman from DeKalb County had stopped. The sight of the cross had brought conviction to his heart, but it took him 30 minutes to verbalize his need. Pulling out my small pocket New Testament and a gospel booklet, we read some wonderful salvation verses together. I then showed Arnold a prayer he could pray to ask Jesus into his heart. Gently, I invited this grandfather to pray the sinner's prayer with me.

The gray-haired man thought for a long time before speaking. Finally, he said, "I know I'm going to hell if I don't accept Jesus' love for me, but I just can't do it. I can't pray that prayer."

I was stunned! I reminded Arnold of his grandchildren he sat with in church and how he would certainly want to be with them in heaven. Arnold abruptly said he needed to go, that he was late for his morning coffee with his friends at the little café up the road. Interestingly, he invited me to join him and his friends.

Forty-five minutes later, I walked my way up to the small-town diner. Arnold gladly introduced me to his six coffee-drinking buddies. We talked for a few minutes, and then most of the men left, leaving only Arnold, me, and his best friend sitting at a long table.

I quickly shifted the conversation to spiritual matters again. Thomas, Arnold's best friend, was equally troubled to learn that his friend was not saved.

"Arnold, you and I have sat in this same café for 10 years and have drunk coffee, and we've talked about everything in the world, including church, every week. I thought you were saved this whole time!"

Thomas and I together shared the gospel with Arnold once more. We also presented him with the sinner's prayer again. With tears in his eyes, Thomas begged his friend to go ahead and get things right with the Lord. We noted that no one else was in the restaurant except a lone waitress wiping down tables at the far end. I didn't see how in the world Arnold could possibly refuse our offer to accept Christ this time.

But he did refuse.

My conversation with Arnold haunted me for weeks, even though I had many positive conversations with people in this county. I would wake up in night sweats. Even years later I woke up with a jolt, thinking about Arnold going to hell.

Chapter Seven

BLOOD AND JOY

WALKER COUNTY:
JANUARY 1997 TO APRIL 1997

Introduction

I was anxious to begin walking in the coal-mining communities of Walker County where I had attended high school three decades earlier. But as I walked the narrow roads of Walker County, I kept dodging mammoth coal trucks speeding by. The shoulders of the roads were so deep in coal soot that I purchased black tennis shoes and black jeans so I would look clean even when I wasn't. Surprisingly, I continued to meet people whom I remembered, or who remembered me, from my teenage days at Walker County High School and Westside Baptist Church, both in Jasper.

Yerkwood Camp

A man named Bruce pulled over one day in his vehicle, walked up to me, and immediately began speaking in another language. He then said in English, "Let me interpret what I believe the Spirit of God is saying to you: God will soon ask you to do something you have not done before. Don't be afraid!"

A week later I was walking south of the small town of Dora. About 10 different people over a two-day period warned me not to walk into the old coal-mining community of Yerkwood Camp, which was located up the road. Some of these warnings even came from men who lived in Yerkwood Camp. More than one person said to me, "Don't walk into our community to visit us—we are too messed up!" Never before or since have I had another community say that to me.

With each new warning I asked additional questions. From what I was told, Yerkwood Camp had, in recent years, been de-annexed from the town of Dora. It seemed the local police were no longer willing to patrol Yerkwood Camp because of the heavy cocaine use and related violence. I was also told that even the dogs were shot up with cocaine in order to prevent outsiders from intruding. That thought sent shivers up my spine.

After the local law enforcement officers refused to go into Yerkwood Camp, the responsibility reverted to the sheriff's department who, in turn, deferred it to the Alabama Highway Patrol. Also, I was told that someone had been shot in Yerkwood Camp just a few days earlier.

I had been walking with the cross full-time for about a year and a half, and God had increasingly given me a burden for the rough places in Alabama. I also remembered Bruce's prophesy from the week before: "Don't be afraid." But the thought of those cocaine-injected dogs still gave me great concern.

I prayed for two days before entering Yerkwood Camp. With the cross on my shoulder, I walked down the long entrance of Yerkwood Camp to a small intersection. From that vantage point I could see about a dozen men in the distance waiting for me around an old pickup truck parked under a big oak tree. I walked up to the group and, after introductions, they informed me they had been waiting for the cross to arrive for two days. The eyes of the men were bloodshot from drugs and alcohol, but their minds seemed curious about the cross.

For an hour I talked, preached, discussed and challenged these men from God's Word. God stirred in their hearts enough that several of the men accepted Bibles and gospel literature.

I spent time walking the roads in the camp that day. The houses were in terrible shape, and I often saw men staggering down the rough streets out of their minds on drugs. In the following days I did my best to get a Bible study started in Yerkwood Camp, but to no avail.

One day as I drove into the camp to meet someone, I saw a large, white dog with blood splattered all over its body. I recoiled at the sight! In the days that followed, the sight of this dog lingered in my mind, and I began to visualize this sight as the spiritual condition of the camp—Satan tearing away at a man's flesh. The following words of Jesus came to my mind: "The thief comes only to steal and kill and destroy; I have come that they may have life, and have it to the full" (John 10:10).

I felt a tension within my own heart about the area. On one hand, I thanked the Lord for protecting me while I walked in Yerkwood Camp. But on the other hand, my heart went out to these people in bondage, and I struggled with the idea of leaving them behind. Previously, I had ministered to communities by Bible study if someone opened up their home, yard, or business for meetings. That opportunity never opened up there and, in the end, I reluctantly traveled on.

The Philippian Jailer Story

I had been walking in Walker County for about five or six weeks, but I had little spiritual results to show for it. One day the Lord prompted me to start telling the story of the Philippian jailer from Acts 16. I was very surprised by the results. On several occasions tough men broke down and started crying!

In this particular Bible story, the apostle Paul and his partner, Silas, were severely beaten and unjustly thrown into prison. The Lord caused a great earthquake, and the jailhouse doors flung open. This story takes place during Roman times, and under Roman law a jailer, without exception, would lose his life if he lost a prisoner. When the jailer saw the prison doors open, he drew his sword to kill himself, thinking his prisoners had surely fled.

However, Paul and Silas called out and assured the jailer they had stayed around to talk with him. The jailer was so moved in his spirit he asked what is still the world's most life-changing question: "Sirs, what must I do to be saved?" (v. 30).

Paul and Silas replied simply: "Believe in the Lord Jesus, and you will be saved—you and your household. Then they spoke the word of the Lord to him and to all the others in his house" (vv. 31, 32).

After Paul and Silas spoke to the jailer's household, the jailer was filled with compassion and washed their wounds. Believing in Jesus, the jailer and his family were then baptized. Next, he brought his new friends into his house and prepared a meal for them. Then comes my favorite part of the story: "The jailer . . .

was filled with joy because he had come to believe in God—he and his whole family" (v. 34).

After telling this story, I asked several men if I could start a Bible study in their home with them and their family. One man said to me in tears, "This is what my family and I need!" Another man said between sobs, "I read that story myself just last night!"

The Lord began to open Bible studies almost every day for several weeks in towns and communities all across Walker County—Jasper, Carbon Hill, Dora, Empire, Parrish, Sipsey, Cordova, Goodsprings and Sumiton. Because I was so excited about what the Lord was doing, I expanded my efforts in walking and talking. After walking long and hard each day, I taught Bible studies in the afternoons and evenings.

The weeks referenced above were such a spiritual blessing to me, and I will never forget those precious times. However, with the blessing came a challenge. I became so physically and emotionally exhausted that I was easily upset at home by anything that didn't go my way. I had nothing left in my emotional tank when I arrived home.

This situation robbed me of some of the joy of the exciting things happening on the streets. Therefore, I had to rethink the whole ministering process and learn to better pace myself physically, emotionally and spiritually.

Chapter Eight

TOUGH CHALLENGES

CULLMAN COUNTY:
JUNE 1997 TO AUGUST 1997

Introduction

The city of Cullman is a very clean community with a strong German influence. I remember a bakery downtown that stirred up my own German heritage and appetite for great breads and pastries. Beside the city of Cullman, the rest of the county is comprised of small communities, rolling hills, and lots of hay fields.

White City

On my second day of walking in Cullman County, a police officer from the small town of Hanceville stopped by. He asked a unique question—one I had never been asked before: "Are you walking with that cross of your own free will?"

The officer then explained that Hanceville had a number of hate-group members, especially in one community appropriately named White City. The policeman further explained that White City was the location of the annual statewide hate-group rally held every July. I thought to myself, *Here I go again—with the men with white gowns and cone hoods.*

The officer then surprised me by saying, "I think you should walk in the White City area. They need something spiritual like this there." After the officer left, I thanked the Lord for telling me so much about the spiritual condition of this county.

The next day I had a conversation with a man named Tommy in another county. I mentioned my conversation from the day before with the Hanceville police officer. Tommy responded, "I was once in that hate-group organization myself, and I know several of those guys in the White City area." This short conversation with Tommy confirmed what the police officer had said about White City.

I had no idea what to expect when I first started walking in White City. But for the next three days, I walked 26 miles alone in this rural community (not a city at all) named for the race of people who lived there. I walked every road, walking some roads several times.

I met many people in White City, and I had many polite conversations about Christ. My desire was to start a Bible study in a nonbeliever's home in the community. I focused my conversations on Jesus and His love. If I saw someone too far away to speak conversationally, I yelled out, "Think of Jesus today!" I had been walking in the daytime, as I always do, and in the light of day all appeared somewhat normal. But I knew better.

One day I met a man who wanted to really talk. He confirmed the presence of the hate-group rallies in the neighborhood. He even attended once with his cousin out of curiosity. "I was appalled at the men I recognized there," he said. "I had no idea all these men were mixed up in this. Outstanding citizens from Cullman whom I had known for years were present. I was so shocked I never attended again."

My heart was broken for this community and county. These hate groups and their related events cast long shadows. As a result, almost no African Americans lived in Cullman County. I fully expected to have a major confrontation with this hate group as I walked in the county. As a consequence, I felt uneasy in my spirit for the entire two-and-a-half months I walked there. But God was teaching me to do battle in the Spirit realm with prayer. I never drive through Cullman County without sending up a prayer of reconciliation for these people toward God and their fellowman. I am reminded of the following verse from Scripture: "For our struggle is not against flesh and blood, but against the rulers, against the authorities, against the powers of this dark world and against the spiritual forces of evil in the heavenly realms" (Ephesians 6:12).

A Life Saved

My daughter, Autumn (age 13 at the time), was walking with me one day in downtown Cullman as a special treat to her dad. We had a good day walking, and we were able to talk with a number of people about the Lord, including a man named Marvin. Marvin managed a local business in town, but he took the time to hear our story about Jesus' death on the cross as payment for our sins. Marvin then prayed the sinner's prayer as he asked Jesus into his heart.

Marvin immediately told his friends of his new relationship with Christ. The following week I had a Bible study with him as I usually do when a man accepts the Lord. He told me about his friends' response to his new faith: "Some guy walking down the road with a cross and then praying with you cannot possibly do you any good."

Marvin responded, "Oh yes, it is doing me some good. I can feel the difference inside me, and I'm acting different on the outside."

Later Marvin told me, "All this movement in my life toward God started when you walked in Huntsville last year, and I first saw the cross." This statement encouraged me greatly.

The following week I had another Bible study with Marvin. He told me of a major confrontation he had with another man a few days earlier. He said, "If it hadn't been for these recent spiritual changes in my life, I probably would have killed that man this weekend!"

I drove home that evening thinking about Marvin's comments and how another man had been saved—this time physically—because of the power of the cross.

A Special Day in Colony

Colony is a very small African-American community in the far southwest corner of Cullman County. I had my eye on this community ever since I talked with the Hanceville police officer. It was a hot and humid day in late July when I walked my way toward Colony.

In the weeks prior, I almost did not make it back to my truck on a couple occasions. I remember one 96-degree day when I just stared at my truck from two blocks away as I stood under a tree—I couldn't walk any more. On a couple other occasions, I collapsed after reaching my truck, unable to make another move.

Obviously, I was still learning to listen to my own body and understand when it had reached its limits. I ended up in the hospital late one night in terrible pain with what I later learned were kidney stones. After that experience I began to ease off somewhat from walking in the heat of the day. But I still didn't realize how much I needed to adjust my routine in extreme heat.

I felt fine as I started walking toward the little community of Colony. However, my body tired after just a few miles. I turned off state Highway 91 onto the horseshoe loop that winds through the neighborhood. At the small city hall I stopped for a much-needed glass of water. While there, I met Earleen Johnson, Colony's African-American mayor. Earleen was a retired schoolteacher, and I asked her how she became mayor of Colony. She said, "I had no thought of running for mayor, but some drug dealers were seeking the office, and that concerned me. One day as I was reading in 1 or 2 Samuel, the Lord spoke to me. I read the words, 'you will have a fair rule.' So I ran for office and was elected."

Earleen and I talked for a while before praying together for the county. She asked me a lot of questions about the cross walk. The mayor said, "There are only about 500 blacks who live in Cullman County out of a total population of 70,000. Of these 500 people, about 350 live here in Colony. The rest live in the city of Cullman. Few, if any, of my folks live out in the country by themselves, except around here. And this community was not always in Cullman County. Many decades ago the county line near here was redrawn, and Colony became part of Cullman County."

She and I then prayed for all the people of Cullman County—for Colony, Cullman, Hanceville, White City, and all the little communities out in the country. I seldom experience the power of God in prayer as I did that day in Colony. I prayed God's blessings and favor for Earleen; she prayed God's blessings and protection for me. As I left city hall Earleen told me, "God sent you here today."

Spiritually, I was floating after talking with Earleen. But I was surprised that my body still seemed so sluggish. Some time later, after my seventh mile walking, I was so exhausted by the heat and humidity that I began to cry out to the Lord in great earnest for help. I had already consumed several drinks, but I needed more. Immediately, a man walked out of his house with a large glass of water. I drank half the water and then poured the other half over my head. After thanking the man, I continued down the road.

I had not walked another 100 yards when I cried out to the Lord again in sheer desperation, "Lord, I'm in serious trouble. I need big help!" Honestly I didn't even know what to pray for, and I was shocked that the last gift of water had not helped at all. I just knew my body felt terrible all over, and my head felt like it was on fire from the inside out. I had never felt this way before, and I knew this sensation was not good.

A minute later I was suddenly hit with rain so hard and fast I could not see straight. It literally took my breath away. I felt like I was being beaten to a pulp by the water. And it was cold! The best news was that I began to feel life returning to my body.

With every step I felt more refreshed. I uttered praise after praise to the Lord. I just couldn't believe what the Lord was doing for me!

I walked the last mile to my truck. I pulled my shirt off and shivered as the cold rain hit my back. I jumped inside the cab, dried off my face, and pulled on a dry shirt. My truck was parked in the grass parking lot of a little country church. As I pulled out of the driveway, I rolled the window down because it had suddenly stopped raining.

Driving the 60 miles back to Birmingham, I was taken aback to see that the wet pavement was only in the section of road I had just walked!

This is a file photo of me walking a stretch of road with the cross.

Chapter Nine

RESURRECTION POWER

Introduction

Talladega County is best known for the NASCAR track at Talladega Superspeedway, which is located between Birmingham and the Alabama-Georgia state line on Interstate 20. While the superspeedway and the city of Talladega are located in the northern part of the county, the towns of Childersburg and Sylacauga are located toward the southern end of this long and narrow county. Very small rural communities make up the remainder of this lovely county.

Prayer Partner

For the first time in my cross walk ministry, I asked an in-county friend of mine, Daron Limbaugh, from Childersburg, to be my weekly prayer partner. Daron and I met each week while I walked in this county, and we had great prayer times together for the people of Talladega County. This started a practice that has continued for many years—having a prayer partner who actually lives in the county where I am walking. With Daron and I praying together weekly for the county, and each praying separately every day, the cross walk took a step forward spiritually.

Connie and I were constantly in prayer, day and night, for the county I was walking in. Many other friends were also praying for our street ministry. But having an in-county prayer partner allowed our prayers to be much more specific because my prayer partner often knew the groups of people, the culture, and sometimes the actual families with whom we were dealing.

I am reminded of the story of Nehemiah in the Old Testament when Nehemiah made the men of Jerusalem rebuild the section of the wall surrounding the city closest to their own homes. The same idea that works with rebuilding a security wall also works with prayer—we protect best that which is closest to us. Therefore, a man who lives in the county I'm walking in has a vested interest in praying with me and seeing spiritual victory accomplished.

Resurrection Power

I was thinking about the resurrection power of Jesus that is available to us as Christians, so I began talking about this subject in one of the towns. I met a man named Wayne, who worked in a funeral home, and I shared my thoughts with him about this resurrection power. I told Wayne that this power was also available to him.

Wayne asked me, "Paul, if I accept Jesus, these dead bodies around here won't start moving around, will they?"

The next time I met Wayne for Bible study, the subject of resurrection power was still on my mind. I stressed to Wayne that God's power was limitless in our lives if we had sufficient faith. To illustrate this point, I referred a couple of times to the dead forms in the funeral home that day. Finally, I said, "Wayne, if you and I had the proper faith, we could lay our hands on these dead bodies now, and they would come back to life."

Wayne quickly replied in a most serious manner, "Oh, Paul, please don't do that—these funerals have already been paid for!"

What Wayne didn't understand was that dead people coming back to life was not the problem. The problem was living people acting as though they were dead.

Later, I had another conversation about resurrection power. Mike, a high school principal, told me a story about his mother's question to him about life after death. He was by his mother's side as she was on her deathbed.

"Mike, what's going to happen to me when I die—where am I going?"

Mike said to me, "I had three college degrees at the time, but I had no answer to my mother's question."

Mike found a Bible in the hospital room and read the whole New Testament. A few days later, the hospital chaplain led Mike to the Lord. Mike was then able to answer his mother's question and talk about the resurrection of the saints to heaven, resulting in his mother also believing in Jesus. Mike's mother then experienced the assurance that she, too, was going to heaven when she died.

I found one community in Talladega County, however, that was *not* interested in discussing resurrection power. Several people spoke to me about this rural community leading to Lake Hypatia, and I made plans to walk there. Many of those who lived in this community were Satan-worshipers. Also, very large satanic conferences were held on this site from time to time, with people coming from all over to take part in satanic rituals.

I was extremely disappointed to learn we had such demonic places in Alabama. I prayed for several days before walking in this evil place. I read and quoted Scripture all day as I walked through this community. Although I did not have any conversations, I walked the quiet and shadowy loop that leads through this area. Several people peered at me through their house windows, but no one ventured out for a conversation. I continued to pray for this community.

A week later, on Halloween day, Connie and I drove through this community again and attached gospel booklets to all the newspaper boxes or mailboxes. I am reminded of Jesus' words in the following verse that had been on my mind during those many weeks in Talladega County: "I am the resurrection and the life. He who believes in me will live, even though he dies; and whoever lives and believes in me will never die. Do you believe this?" (John 11:25, 26).

Chapter Ten

SPIRITUAL GRIDIRON

Introduction

Tuscaloosa County could be called the "University of Alabama County" because the school dominates every phase of life here. Actually, I should say that football dominates every phase of life. As much as I personally love college football, I was happy to be walking during the off-season so that spiritual conversations could also be entertained.

My prayer partner here was Eddie McKnight, a businessman, who has been my friend for decades. God greatly used Eddie's prayers in this county. We met weekly at his office and prayed for changed lives.

Soup and Cornbread

It rained nearly every day during the month of January. I had walked in the rain many times before, but never day after day like what I experienced here. I was dripping wet one day, and a man in a big truck stopped and handed me a large cup of steaming-hot soup and a piece of cornbread wrapped in wax paper. Several people were standing on the porch of a house nearby and saw the trucker's kind deed.

I had the cross on my shoulder, the soup in one hand and the cornbread in the other. I was in a real bind trying to juggle my newly offered treasures, which smelled so good. So, I walked up to the porch where the people were watching, propped my cross up against the rails, and opened the lid to my soup while standing in the pouring-down rain.

My audience invited me onto the porch, but I was too muddy and wet, and I didn't want to mess up their nice house or porch. So the men quickly found a spoon for my soup, and the ladies made me a cup of coffee. They stood there and watched me eat, and each one asked me questions.

For three months I continued to pray for one of the men, Robert, who was on the porch. One day the Lord led me across his path again at his job site, and there Robert accepted the Lord. All this started with a cup of soup and cornbread. In the Book of John, Jesus says several times, "I am the bread of life." Perhaps here in the Deep South, Jesus would have said, "I am the cornbread of life!"

Conversations on the Streets

Many people started conversations about the cross or made comments about it while I was walking in Tuscaloosa County. Here are several that I documented:

- While walking by a small auto-repair shop, I offered the owner a gospel booklet. He took one look at the cross and then yelled out, "There is no heaven or hell! We humans have seen as far as Mars, and no hell has been found!" He became very upset and marched off to his home, which was located next to his shop. I never had a moment to respond.

- One day I stopped to rest as I was carrying the cross. A lady and a 7-year-old boy named Joshua came running out of a nearby house to greet me. The mother told of Joshua seeing the cross six weeks earlier while using his field glasses (he had seen the cross from half a mile away). Joshua immediately began drawing and coloring a picture of Jesus carrying His cross. The boy and his mom had saved the work of art in hopes they would see me again. It touched my heart as Joshua presented me with his beautiful handiwork.

- I spent an hour one day talking with a man named Johnny. He kept saying to me, "I sense that I am an angel." Finally, I addressed his comment by saying, "Johnny, I strongly sense that you are not an angel. Make plans to carry on with your life."

- A personal testimony was given to me one day from a man in Tuscaloosa. He told of an experience he'd had in the early '60s: "One night I was suddenly awakened. I turned over and was terrified to find a casket beside my bed! I looked inside the casket, and my own body was inside. After a while the casket went away, but I remained awake all night thinking about my sins. Two weeks later I went to church, and there I got saved!"

University Mound

In the center of the University of Alabama's campus is the traditional college quadrangle (or "Quad," as it's usually called) with trees and open, grassy spaces. The library and various classrooms are positioned around the perimeter. Denny Chimes tower is also located in this area. Additionally situated within the Quad is a rectangle-shaped earthen mound the size of a house foundation. A house had actually been located on the site approximately 150 years ago. But when the house came down, the flat, 3-foot-high mound became a favorite speaking site on campus. Several busy sidewalks run below and adjacent to the mound, bringing speakers and students together.

The Holy Spirit led me to spend a week at the mound. I propped my cross up on top and, with Bible in hand, I read aloud from Scripture each day for the first three days. First I read John, then Matthew, and then Luke. I had been prompted by the Holy Spirit in the past year to read Scripture in public. This little-heeded verse had first gotten my attention: "Devote yourself to the public reading of Scripture, to preaching and to teaching" (1 Timothy 4:13).

On the third day Connie came with me and sang from the mound. I can't describe to you what a blessing it was to hear the resounding words of "Amazing Grace," "The Blood Will Never

Lose Its Power," and the old-time spiritual "Swing Low, Sweet Chariot." Connie's voice carried much better than expected and reverberated off the surrounding classrooms. The students really seemed to enjoy the singing too.

I was surprised at how polite and shy the UA students were toward us. I expected to be heckled a bit, but the students showed a surprising amount of Southern hospitality toward us.

The last two days I stood below the mound speaking to students for hours on end. This process worked well since the students were now accustomed to seeing the cross and were curious about our message. Several students mentioned they had already seen the cross in their hometown. From this point forward, the Lord gave me a heart to minister on college and university campuses in Alabama at every opportunity.

*Here I am reading Scripture at the Mound on the University of Alabama campus.
I spent a week around this mound talking with students.*

Antichrist

I met a man named Roger one day as I was walking in Tuscaloosa. Roger seemed overly concerned about my safety as I walked. He urged me over and over again not to walk the section of road ahead. Finally, I told Roger in a confident voice that I was going to walk the road ahead and that I would trust God to help me as He had done so many times before.

Minutes later I learned more about Roger's true motive. Two women stepped up to the cross to join our conversation. After introductions, Roger asked if he could speak. His whole demeanor began to change as he looked at the cross with contempt. He began to condemn me for carrying the cross and for telling people about Jesus and the Bible, which he called "all lies."

"Furthermore," Roger stated, "This man needs to be talking about *me* on the streets because I'm the Antichrist, and I'm the one people need to know about!"

The two women and I looked at Roger in shock. One of the women immediately began rebuking Roger in the name of the Lord Jesus Christ. A very lively discussion ensued. I shared Scripture with Roger and prayed that his eyes would be opened. I knew Roger was not the Antichrist, but he did have the spirit of the antichrist within him.

We eventually parted ways, and I began to walk the stretch of road that Roger had urged me not to walk. I encountered seven highway construction workers waiting for some equipment to arrive. I presented the gospel to these men as a group. I even gave an invitation for salvation—just like in church—but no one responded.

My conversation with the man who called himself the Antichrist was still rolling over and over in my mind. Therefore, I shared this story with the highway construction crew. I concluded my remarks by saying, "It's just occurred to me as I speak that you have two spiritual choices. You can choose the Lord Jesus Christ, who I've just told you about, or you can choose the Antichrist—*whom do you choose?*"

A man named Napoleon quickly stepped forward at this second invitation saying, "If that's the two choices I have, I want to take a stand for Jesus!" Napoleon bowed his head and prayed the sinner's prayer out loud as I led the way. Napoleon's coworkers looked on with wonder at Napoleon's boldness.

For days after this incident, I talked on the streets about our two spiritual choices—the Lord Jesus Christ, or the Antichrist. I found this interesting verse: "Dear children, this is the last hour; and as you have heard that the antichrist is coming, even now many antichrists have come. This is how we know it is the last hour" (1 John 2:18).

Chapter Eleven

DIVINE
APPOINTMENTS

TUSCALOOSA COUNTY:
JANUARY 1998 TO APRIL 1998

Danny Killed

One day I had a 6:30 a.m. Bible study meeting scheduled in Tuscaloosa at a church construction site. To meet this commitment, I set my alarm for 4 a.m. Connie's sleeping routine had recently been out of sync, and I hated to awaken her needlessly. But my alarm went off as scheduled and, as I was dressing, I made the following comment to my wife: "I doubt these construction workers will show up on time for this early-morning Bible study, but I feel I should try. It's hard to determine if this interruption to you and the girls is worthwhile. Only God knows."

I arrived at the construction site on time for the Bible study, but the men I expected to meet weren't there. However, I did meet a new man on the premises named Danny, who had shown up very early for his first day at work. This very likable 26-year-old and I struck up a conversation, and I quickly started witnessing to a spiritually hungry soul. An hour later Danny accepted the Lord Jesus into his heart.

In the next 40 days I saw Danny many times. I stopped by his job site on several occasions. Danny and I also met twice for Bible study at his apartment, and we had a third meeting scheduled. The Holy Spirit stirred in my heart to review the salvation message with Danny each time I saw him, even though he had already made a commitment to the Lord. The verses below are the primary scriptures I detailed in my journal that Danny and I studied:

- John 1:1-4—Jesus is God, and He created all things.
- Hebrews 1:2, 3—God has spoken to us through Jesus.
- John 3:1-16—God loves you. Believe in Jesus.
- Romans 3:23—All people have sinned.
- Romans 6:23—Our reward is death; God's gift is life.
- Ephesians 2:8, 9—Salvation is by faith, not by good works.
- Romans 10:9—Confess "Jesus is Lord" and believe.
- Revelation 3:20—God is knocking at our heart's door.
- 1 John 1:9—When we sin, confess our sin to God.
- Acts 19:1-10—Pray for the Holy Spirit.

On a Sunday afternoon I drove to Tuscaloosa to meet with Danny again. As I approached Danny's apartment door, I was informed that he had been shot and killed just hours earlier! I was horrified.

I didn't know any of Danny's family or where they lived. For that matter, I didn't even know Danny very well. So, I talked with several people in the apartment building for a little while and then left for home. Before I left, however, two young boys accepted the Lord after hearing about Danny's decision for Christ.

Danny

Danny's Funeral

Several days later I was in a small church in a poor area of town for Danny's funeral. The place was overflowing with sobbing family members and friends. There was much emotion. Several women fainted and had to be carried out of the hot building. One young man had to be carried out of the church by four men as he screamed at the top of his lungs. I understood—friends and family should never die young. I cried through the whole service for this man I barely knew. I had no idea who any of these people were; all I knew was that they were hurting. The dear, elderly pastor spoke to the living, trying his best to direct those who remained to a future in heaven.

After the service, and just before the funeral procession began, the pastor motioned me over and asked, "I guess you were Danny's boss at work?"

"No, sir," I replied, "I'm the man who walks with the Jesus cross in Alabama, and I had the privilege of leading Danny to the Lord a month ago. Danny's in heaven!" The dear pastor dropped his head to the steering wheel of his vehicle and lifted his hands upward as he sobbed for relief and joy. With that, the motorcade drove off to the grave site.

I was shaken emotionally by the events of those last several days. As I drove home I prayed, thanking the Lord for helping me finish the job with Danny. Little did I know the job was only beginning!

The Tug of the Holy Spirit

Danny was buried the Saturday before Palm Sunday, and I had a hard time getting this young man off my mind. I continued to travel to Danny's hometown because I was asked to take part in an Easter drama. Being the week of Easter, I was busy with drama practice every day and memorizing lines. Acting was something brand-new to me. Naturally, I was very nervous about the event. I was also determined to spend quality time walking on the streets of Tuscaloosa every day during the Easter week. However, the Holy Spirit kept bringing my mind back to Danny.

Driving to Tuscaloosa County the Monday of Easter week, I felt a strong tugging in my chest that I couldn't ignore. I remember saying out loud to the Lord, "I don't know what else to do about Danny. I witnessed the best I could to him, he accepted you into his heart, and I attended his funeral. What else could I possibly do?"

Later that morning I drove past Danny's old job site. I pulled over and walked into the boss's office at the construction site. Minutes later I was having breakfast with Danny's former boss in a local restaurant. An hour later, he bowed his head and accepted Jesus into his heart. The boss then made a very forward-thinking comment when he lifted his head. "I believe God wants me to reach my employees."

The next day, Tuesday, the boss paid his employees' wages while they listened to me speak in the half-completed church building (now that doesn't happen often). I stood where I thought the podium would eventually be set, and the 20 construction workers sat on piles of lumber and other materials and listened. I told of Danny dying and going to heaven 40 days after his decision for Christ. I then told of Jesus' ascension to heaven 40 days after His resurrection.

I gave an invitation to accept Jesus, and four men boldly came forward and stood facing the others. With tears in their eyes, they prayed the sinner's prayer with me. I then spoke to them about a follow-up Bible study, just as I had with the boss the day before.

The Lord wouldn't leave me alone about Danny. I walked in the community surrounding the church where Danny's funeral had been held. I met many individuals and told them Danny's story. After this, the only people possibly left for me to meet were Danny's family, if he had any. Such emotion and commotion had flowed at the funeral that day that I was unable to determine who the family was.

I said to the Lord one day in prayer, "If You want me to speak with Danny's family, You need to provide me the phone number." A short time later a man walked up to me on the street and told me Danny's mother's phone number.

Danny's mom could hardly believe my story about meeting Danny and talking with him about the Lord before his death. I asked this grieving woman if Danny had any family members other than her. I was surprised when she told me that Danny had eight brothers and sisters, many with spouses, and several nieces and nephews. I asked her to get the family together the next evening, which was Good Friday.

It was a very emotional meeting with Danny's family. I told about my encounter with Danny and how he had come to know the Lord. His family and I agreed to continue meeting on a regular basis. These Bible studies continued for eight months, during which time I met countless family members and friends, and many made decisions for Christ.

I'll never forget visiting Danny's mom unannounced one afternoon several years later. As I entered her living room, I saw Danny's picture on the mantel and my picture next to his. Seeing those two pictures together was an unexpected blessing. But what if I had not gotten up at 4 a.m. the day I met Danny? What if I had not followed up with him and his family and friends?

I was just beginning to understand the idea that sometimes we have "only today" with a person or with a community.

Only today!

Chapter Twelve

TORNADO TALES

JEFFERSON COUNTY:
APRIL 1998 TO MAY 1998

Introduction

O n April 8, 1998, an F-5 (the highest level) tornado ripped through parts of Alabama, doing extreme damage in Tuscaloosa, St. Clair and Jefferson counties. Jefferson County was the hardest hit, with several dozen people killed and hundreds of homes literally blown off the face of the earth. The twister struck at the very heart of the following five western Jefferson County communities:

- Edgewater
- McDonald Chapel
- Pratt City
- Rock Creek
- Sylvan Springs

Alabama has seldom seen a tornado so powerful. The Lord moved on my heart to start walking in these troubled areas, but I waited until all the roads were opened. By this time the National Guard, the initial crowd of volunteers, and the media were gone. The survivors were left with the remaining devastation and all the interrelated issues of piecing life back together.

My prayer partners for this ministry area were Carl Sr. and Violet Dickinson, dear saints who lived across the street from us. This older couple took an unusual interest in my family and ministry. Most warm afternoons when I arrived home, Carl would be sitting under a shade tree in his front lawn. Pulling up another chair, he'd invite me to join him for conversation. I would tell Carl and Violet about the events of my day (including most of the stories in this book). Until the Lord called them home, these two fervent prayer warriors prayed faithfully for hundreds of people by name that I met along the way in the first several years of the cross walk.

Reading Scripture

Everywhere I walked in these five decimated communities I felt a sense of sorrow and confusion. The sights, smells and miseries of death and destruction spanned for miles, with piles of debris everywhere. Everything that remained after the storm was twisted together like spaghetti—mangled vehicles, fallen trees, splinters of lumber and furniture, shreds of clothing and trash. The area was far from quiet. The sounds of chain saws and hammers filled the air.

But there was also a sense of reverence in the air. I use the word *reverence* because I was able to read Scripture with people openly. I read Bible verses to construction crews, machine operators, traffic police, utility workers, truck drivers, government workers and, most importantly, homeowners. People were hurting!

Construction crews stopped working and allowed me to read the Bible and pray. Conversations stopped, and people turned to talk about the cross and let me read to them. I have never experienced another time like this in which I was so free to read God's Word with people. Often I read the following verses and then explained the meaning: "Humble yourselves, therefore, under God's mighty hand, that he may lift you up in due time. Cast all your anxiety on him because he cares for you" (1 Peter 5:6, 7).

I would explain *there are times when God wants us to focus on Him and put Him first in our lives.* As we focus on God and give Him our full attention, He lifts us out of our misery and anxiety. God truly does care for all of us!

Unforgettable Sights and Stories

Survival stories were often the subject of initial conversations with homeowners. Three people told of surviving in a bathtub while their house was being torn away. A husband and wife told of crawling under their front concrete steps as their house completely disappeared. Another man told of his 90-year-old aunt changing chairs in her living room because she was getting wet, not realizing the roof had been blown off her house.

One of the sights from my first week walking in the McDonald Chapel area nearly drove me crazy. I passed an intact home with an attached carport. Everything about the house was in good repair, without a visible problem anywhere. A man with a leaf blower was meticulously blowing away a handful of leaves left on the driveway. I stared in disbelief as I looked around at the contrasting scenes.

The homes on either side were totally and utterly destroyed. As far as the eye could see, there was complete devastation. On an adjacent lot, a crushed vehicle had landed upside down on what had been the foundation of someone's home. Yet there was this man, slowly blowing leaf by leaf from the driveway of an intact home. His actions were inconsistent with the reality that surrounded him.

I approached the man, not knowing what to say. So I let him talk. He told me he had come over to check on an elderly widow and stayed to clean her yard. His explanation made reasonable sense, yet it took months for me to get this odd picture out of my mind.

I was confused as to why this picture (a man ignoring major sorrow around him in order to solve petty problems) troubled me so in light of this man's reasonable explanation. Then the truth hit me. How often had I seen only the small picture of my

This picture was taken adjacent to an undamaged house where a man was blowing a few leaves from a driveway.

own life and ignored the larger reality of others around me—their hurts, their miseries, their poverty, and their plight in life?

Oh, Lord, please help me to see the bigger picture of Your will for my life; help me to see the needs of others!

Everything Lost

I stood in front of what had once been a man's house in the community of Edgewater. Absolutely nothing was left of the home. Behind where the residence had once stood, several vehicles were piled on top of one another, crushed. I asked the homeowner to share his story with me.

"The wind was blowing very hard against my house, and I began to realize that I might not make it through the storm alive," the man explained. "I ran outside and dove underneath a large tree that had fallen over a shallow ditch across the street. Soon afterward, my house exploded as it blew away. I felt as if my flesh was being torn away from my bones by the extremely high wind. I could see the meat on my cheek bones being pulled in front of my face! I felt sure that I would die! But somehow I survived. Today I have nothing left—neither my house nor any of my four vehicles were insured."

After more conversation I turned the discussion to spiritual matters. I shared a number of scriptures with this gentleman, and then I asked if he wanted to have a relationship with the Lord. His reply dumbfounded me as he said, "No, I don't feel God is drawing me."

"Sir," I said, "You've just told of your flesh being almost ripped from your bones! You've lost everything you own! God is the only thing you have left, and He's the most precious thing anyway. Why not accept Him today?"

My plea was to no avail. The man showed no interest in spiritual matters whatsoever, and I was so very disappointed for him. Theologically, though, the man had a point. Unless the Holy Spirit draws on our hearts, we cannot come to the Lord. On the other hand, Scripture says, "Seek the Lord while he may be found; call on him while he is near" (Isaiah 55:6). I walked away thinking this man had truly lost everything. In the old days, perhaps, the following telegram could have been sent: "Everything lost—nothing remains!"

One Page of the Bible

One day a man in Rock Creek told me of his own storm adventure. He said that the morning after the tornado, he crawled out of his hiding place to find his house completely gone. About the only thing that remained was one page from the Bible lying on a bush in his front yard. I asked the man what scripture was on the lost page. He replied, "Hosea 6." However, I continued on my way, speaking to other people.

That evening I suddenly awoke thinking about Hosea 6. I could not remember what was written in that particular chapter, so I turned on my bedside lamp and read the following:

"Come, let us return to the Lord. He has torn us to pieces
but he will heal us; he has injured us but he will bind up our
wounds. After two days he will revive us; on the third day
he will restore us, that we may live in his presence. Let us
acknowledge the Lord; let us press on to acknowledge him.
As surely as the sun rises, he will appear" (vv. 1-3a).

I did not sleep another wink the rest of the night. Instead, I thought about what I had just read. I still reflect on this chapter and, especially, the challenge contained therein: "Let us acknowledge the Lord; let us press on to acknowledge him. As surely as the sun rises, he will appear."

A New Concept

I was still coming to grips with the idea that an individual I had met was later killed, and that was bad enough. But for an entire community to be wiped off the face of the earth was a whole new concept. I was startled by the thought that I could minister in any community in Alabama and, sometime later, that community might be totally destroyed and its citizens lost for eternity. This notion had never entered my mind before, and the visual demonstration of obliteration in these five communities now brought home the fragility of life.

Two years earlier I had walked in two of these five affected communities. A short-lived Bible study had been held in one community in one of the homes that was now destroyed.

A new question gripped my heart as I contemplated walking in future neighborhoods: *If a community is destroyed sometime after I walk and minister there, what spiritual difference will my time there have made in the lives of the people?*

Whoa! With that heavy thought, I headed to Chilton County.

Chapter Thirteen

FRUIT OF
UNFAILING LOVE

CHILTON COUNTY:
JUNE 1998 TO SEPTEMBER 1998

Introduction

C hilton County is famous for its many peach orchards, and this fruit pervades the social and economic base there. Even one of the county's water towers is crafted in the shape of a large Chilton County peach. I ate more peaches the summer I walked there than I had eaten in my whole life, and I enjoyed every single bite!

Many times as I'm walking I talk about a spiritual theme. In this county I chose a scripture about fruit for my theme— Hosea 10:12: "Reap the fruit of unfailing love." I often made the comparison to people I met that fruit trees in this county bear *peaches*. But the cross—also a tree—bore *Jesus*, who is God's "fruit of unfailing love," and who satisfies our every desire.

I also had a personal reason for walking in this county. My parents are both buried in an old cemetery in downtown Clanton. My first day walking there, I started with an emotional prayer time at my parents' graveside as I thanked the Lord for such godly parents. My walking and ministering in this county with a Jesus cross is a lingering testimony to the righteous lives of my parents, Paul Sr. and Mildred Schweigert. They are still bearing spiritual fruit decades after their heavenly homegoing.

I had a wonderful prayer partner in this county named George Champion. I had known George for many years, and he was a longtime resident of Chilton county. His prayers, fasting and meetings with me were invaluable. George had been a pastor for many years, but now he was a representative for a major logging company. With his background, he knew every square inch of the county.

Jack's Fruit Stand

One day I met a man named Jack who was selling fruit out of a new horse trailer under a big oak tree in the old Wal-Mart parking lot in Clanton. We struck up a conversation and a friendship. After several weeks of meeting together, Jack accepted Jesus into his heart. We then began a weekly Bible study session together.

Connie went with me on two occasions and sang a few songs for Jack. On the second occasion she said, "Jack, I woke up this morning singing an old song I haven't heard or sung for several years. I'm not even sure I'll remember all the words. The name of the song is 'Finally Home'[1]. It's actually a funeral song.

---

[1] Don Wyrtzen and L.E. Singer. "Finally Home." Composed by Don Wyrtzen. © 1971 Singspiration Music (administered by Brentwood-Benson Music Publishing, Inc.).

The words are about touching the hand of God when we get to heaven." Connie stood next to U.S. Highway 31, between the watermelons and the cantaloupes, and articulated the words that seemed to come to her as she sang. When Connie finished singing, Jack gave her a big hug, and we said goodbye.

A week later I had a Bible study with a mentally challenged couple in another part of town. This couple was so severely challenged that they were just barely able to live alone. For them, I condensed the words of John 3:16 to just two words: "Jesus loves." I was in the process of explaining these two words when the woman of the house blurted out to me, "Jack is dead!" I asked her why she had said this to me, and she replied, "I don't know."

I quickly excused myself and drove immediately to the local morgue. There, I was informed that my friend, Jack, died two days earlier of a heart attack. Furthermore, his funeral was to be held in a few hours. I was shaken!

I wasn't dressed for a funeral, so I rushed 50 miles home to shower and throw on my sport coat. Then I dashed back to Clanton for the afternoon funeral. After someone realized my spiritual connection to Jack, I was asked to speak at the graveside service. There, I explained our friendship and Jack's conversion to Jesus Christ.

Since Jack had sold fruit, I again talked about the phrase from Hosea that he and I had so often discussed: "Reap the fruit of unfailing love." Sunday afternoon, two days later, I visited every home in Jack's mobile home park. I was able to give each family a Bible in Jack's memory. Many more contacts for Christ were started that day. At the funeral I shared the following seeker's prayer that Jack had prayed:

Dear God,
I know that I am a sinner and that
I need Your forgiveness.
Thank You for Your Son, Jesus, His death on the cross,
and His blood that paid the penalty for all my sin.
I now invite Jesus Christ to come into my heart
and life as my personal Savior.
I desire, by the power of Your Holy Spirit, to turn
away from my sins and toward You for help.
I now allow Jesus Christ to be the leader of my life.
In Jesus' name, amen.

Seventy Bible Studies

The Lord had been opening Bible studies at a rapid pace since the cross walk began. Actually, 70 small Bible studies were started during the first three years. Of these 70, an average of 30 Bible studies continued as I walked among the peach orchards. I had wondered what my saturation point was, and did I ever find out!

Not only did I walk in the heat of Chilton County, but I also taught Bible studies along a 200-mile path from northeast Alabama to west Alabama. Most of these Bible studies met weekly or monthly. I fell exhausted into bed late most nights after walking, teaching and driving 100-300 miles a day. But these were happy days and, besides, I was eating all those good peaches!

I realized I could not continue at this breakneck pace. I began in earnest to close down Bible studies across the state, encouraging new converts to find a church home. I knew this step would not come easy for most individuals. The Lord had called me to individuals and families who were unchurched. Just walking into church for the first time was a major ordeal for most of these dear people, and I realized that many may never cross a church's threshold. Therefore, I had delayed this painful day of cancellation for as long as possible.

What I did not know was that the Lord was preparing me for another major round of Bible studies starting in Chilton County. Each time I cancelled a few Bible studies elsewhere in the state, the same number of Bible study groups immediately started up in Chilton County. This happened numerous times.

During this period in the cross walk, the Lord began teaching me to think long-term by better planning my activities. I gradually restricted my Bible study area to three counties or less and limited each Bible study term to one year. Eventually, the number of ongoing Bible studies I was teaching was reduced from 30 to no more than 10—a more manageable number. However, many times I found saying "goodbye" to be extremely difficult.

New Convert Community

I told my prayer partner one morning that I walked for three days in Maplesville with nothing to show for it, except for the name of a man in the New Convert community who asked me to walk there. After we prayed about the matter, the Lord led me to walk that day in New Convert.

After walking in the community for a while, I began to realize that many families had the same last name as Ace, who had invited me there. I discovered that this was a very old African-American community that had been established over a century ago. Most of the people were, indeed, related to one another.

Ace was unchurched, but he allowed me to start a Bible study in his home. Furthermore, he had a brother who really loved the Lord. After I started walking in the community, Ace's brother offered to walk with me and introduce me to every household. So the two of us walked, talked, and prayed with individuals in every home, listening to their every need. One Sunday my family and I attended the local African-American church, where we met the rest of the community. We were introduced to literally the whole community after meeting Ace and his brother.

An unfortunate incident between a hate group (the guys with hoods and white gowns again) and the New Convert community reared its ugly head as my time in Chilton County neared an end. The African-American teens of the community attended Isabella High School, where a dating issue aroused major racial tensions, spreading throughout the county and the state.

The conflict became a statewide news item involving much controversy, as troublemakers came in from other parts of the state. I tried to be a peacemaker during those anxious days. But by the time the conflict totally settled down, I had already moved on to Autauga County. Throughout those troublesome days, the simple phrase from Hosea kept coming back to my mind: "Reap the fruit of unfailing love. . . ."

Chapter Fourteen

SPIRITUAL HAIRCUTS

Introduction

A utauga County is a bedroom community to Montgomery. In the southern part of the county, many nice subdivisions and golf courses have mushroomed around the county seat of Prattville. However, the remainder of the county is still very rural and sparsely populated.

My prayer partner in this county was a man named Wayne Mushett, a youth pastor in Prattville. We not only had good prayer times together, but Wayne also walked and ministered with me on several occasions. I greatly enjoyed his company.

Living on Nothing, but Having Everything

My prayer partner attended the Prattville Alliance Church (later renamed Fountain of Grace Church), from which the Lord

103

provided many of my prayer partners for the surrounding counties. Most of the people in this church prayed for us on a regular basis. The pastors and the congregation were a tremendous encouragement to my family and me during these early years.

Financially, my family was living on grits and prayer during this time in our ministry. The Lord challenged our hearts to forgo the time and effort necessary to raise funds and to just spend every hour with people on the streets of Alabama.

Our wonderful home church in Birmingham, Metropolitan Church of God, had a food pantry named "Love in Action." We ate from this food pantry for several years until we were financially stable. Sometimes this process was a blow to our college-educated egos, but all this was part of God's school of ministry for us.

People often say to me, "You must be wealthy in order to not work a traditional job." I often reply, "In a sense we are wealthy. We earnestly pray to God, who hears and graciously answers our prayers." We may not have had much money, but God met our every need and many of our desires. Furthermore, we were learning to trust God in bigger and bigger ways for our every need. This lesson alone has become absolutely priceless to each member of my family.

Conversations With Seekers

The following are samples of conversations I had with spiritual seekers in Autauga County:

- I spoke with a man named Jamie one day. He stated that neither he nor his parents had ever gone to church. He had no idea about the meaning of church or the cross. I gladly shared with Jamie the truth about Jesus' death on the cross and the forgiveness that was gained from His shed blood.

- I had breakfast one morning with a man whom I met out in the country. He was highly offended (and became very red in the face) at the idea that we had to choose between good and evil—between Jesus' cross and Satan's evil.

- A man named Bobby said that he didn't go to church and saw no need to. But he read his Bible and prayed every day. I kindly told him that I knew of a very good reason he should go to church—to pay his tithes to the Lord. Bobby was immediately cut to the heart by the Holy Spirit and responded, "That's exactly why I need to be in church, and I promise to start immediately!"

- I spoke with a man named Ricky one day. He had been a Christian for one year, but he received a seven-page letter from a woman who said that if he didn't have the same experience she had, he wasn't saved. I read the letter and shook my head in sadness. I encouraged Ricky to burn the letter and return to the joy he first experienced after accepting the Lord.

- Another man wanted me to give him evidence that there was a God in heaven. I said, "I'll give you five evidential examples as follows:

  1. The Creation
  2. The Bible
  3. The life of Jesus and His disciples
  4. The cross and the empty tomb
  5. The appearances of Jesus after His resurrection."

We then began to talk about one of these.

Courthouse Reading

In several counties before Autauga, I started reading Scripture at each county courthouse. I spent four days in front of the Autauga County courthouse and publicly read through the Gospels of Matthew, Mark, Luke and John. Normally, I read the Gospel of John first at each courthouse because eternal life (3:1-16) and the miracles of Jesus are so clearly communicated. Conversations often started with individuals as I read the Scripture. On other occasions, people just stopped to listen for a few minutes.

At one of these readings Connie sang a song after each chapter I read from the Bible. We handed out gospel booklets to all who walked by. I also propped up the cross nearby because the visual image of the cross is often what people remember.

Barbershops

Before walking in this county, I never considered barbershops a good place for Bible studies. But, as I walked around Prattville with my cross, I constantly darted into barbershops and handed out gospel leaflets.

Once when Connie spent the day with me, we visited people I had met earlier. One of the places we visited was a large barbershop. I asked the owners if Connie could sing for a while. Permission granted, Connie stood up in the middle of this men's barbershop and sang her heart out for about 15 minutes. I could see God working in the hearts of those men as they listened.

When Connie finished singing, I stood and gave an invitation to accept Christ. Several hands lifted in response. After I prayed with these new converts, I suggested we start a weekly Bible study. Everyone agreed, and for the next six months I held a weekly Bible study with the barbers and their customers.

We had a different crowd each week in the barbershop since whoever was getting their hair cut at the time was included in the Bible study. I would stand in the middle of the floor, introduce myself, and then explain about the Bible study that was about to start. I met countless men of the community this way, and a number made decisions for Christ.

Bible studies started in other barbershops. Eventually, I was holding weekly studies in three barbershops in Prattville and one in the countryside. I sometimes smiled at the men in the Bible studies and remarked, "Today you can have your hair cut and your sins removed, all in the same place!"

I really enjoyed my stay in Autauga County. God opened many Bible studies in homes and businesses there. Still, I was itching to get to the capital city of Montgomery. The New Year was upon us, and I felt the Holy Spirit drawing me there with great urgency.

Chapter Fifteen

VISIT WITH
THE GOVERNOR

MONTGOMERY COUNTY:
JANUARY 1999

Introduction

E agerly, I walked in the capital city of Alabama as the
millennium drew to a close. Talk radio and the daily
press were filled with concern about the potential Y2K
problems. Many old computer systems had not been designed
to handle dates past 1999. Scores of people were concerned
about adequate food and water supplies, bank runs on cash,
utility disruptions, and national security issues. Some families
even stored vast supplies of food in apprehension of the new
millennium's beginning.

Actually, people couldn't fully agree as to when the new
1,000-year period began. Did it begin January 1, 2000, or January

1, 2001? A high degree of anxiety was present on many fronts as America entered this new era.

It was in this uncertain environment that I walked for 12 months in the Greater-Montgomery area and into what many people consider the 21st century. Many felt a certain spiritual urgency, or wondering within, particularly if they had little or no spiritual mooring. Would the world come to an end soon? Would aliens invade us? Would the Lord come back again on December 31? Would we have another Great Depression?

My prayer partners in Montgomery County were two siblings named Michael and Lynn Hubbard. These dear people spent every Sunday afternoon for a year in prayer with me in Michael's home for the people of their county.

Prayer With the Governor

As 1999 began, my oldest daughter, Autumn (then age 15), asked me, "Dad, where will you start, and what will you do on your first day in Montgomery?"

I replied straight-faced, "Oh, I'll probably drop by the governor's office and have prayer with Governor Fob James for the city of Montgomery and then just proceed from there!" That comment brought a burst of laughter and teasing from a certain pretty face, and I joined in the laughter myself. A few minutes later I said, "Autumn, seriously, let's not forget that you and I, as Christians, have friends in high places (I pointed upward). If it's God's will, He can move the pieces of life's puzzle around in any way He chooses."

The next morning I walked into the governor's suite in the Alabama State Capitol. I asked the receptionist what it would take for me to visit and have prayer with Gov. James. I was directed to communicate with the governor's appointment secretary, Mr. John Giles. At that moment, Mr. Giles walked up, having just come from the governor's office. Fifteen minutes later I walked out of the state capitol with an appointment for my wife and me to visit the governor.

Two days later Connie and I sat in the receiving room outside the governor's office. While waiting, I spoke with several secretaries who were in the room. I asked the one nearest me if there was anything I could pray with her about. Without hesitating she said, "Oh yes, as you know the governor's term ends in a few days, and I haven't yet found another job. Please pray I'll find one soon so I can continue helping my husband with the mortgage payment." I gladly prayed with this lady.

I then prayed with several others who had similar needs in the room. One of the secretaries mentioned, "Almost everyone left in this building is in the same situation because the new governor, Don Siegelman, will bring in his own staff." Connie and I looked at each other with hearts of compassion and a new sense of purpose. With that, the governor's door opened, and we were ushered in.

I had propped my 12-foot Jesus cross against a tree just outside Gov. James' office. Connie and I stood with the governor, looking out his window at the cross and talking about how Jesus had died for us. We prayed together for the city of Montgomery and the state of Alabama. Then we had our picture taken with him before shaking hands and departing.

Leaving the governor's office, we proceeded to enter office after office on all floors of the Alabama State Capitol. We opened the conversation by saying, "We just had prayer with the governor. Is there anything we can pray with *you* about?" We found many hurting people and several in tears. After praying with everyone we could, we left the state capitol feeling like these prayer sessions were our divine appointment for the day.

Several months later my path crossed the former governor's appointment secretary, Mr. Giles, again. After greetings, he asked me, "Paul, do you realize how you were able to schedule an appointment with Governor Fob James on that particular day? Governor James had just called me into his office to say, 'John, I'm here at the end of my term, and my schedule is light these last couple of weeks. Why don't you fill my calendar up with some of these peons, these little people, who have always wanted to meet the governor, shake his hand, and have their picture taken with him?'"

John continued, "Paul, I walked out of the governor's office, and you were the first peon I saw!" John smiled as he spoke.

Later that afternoon as I was driving home to Birmingham, I was praying and talking to the Lord about my day. Recalling the words of Mr. Giles, I said to the Lord, "That conversation I had this morning was amazing! Lord, if I, the number one peon in all of Alabama, can pray, and You hear my prayer and turn the heart of the king at just the right moment, how much more power would be available to a truly righteous man in the name of Jesus?"

Connie posing with the cross on the lawn of the Alabama State Capitol after we met with Governor Fob James.

Prayer and Anointing

On Sundays I drove to Montgomery to pray for the state and spend time with the Lord. I usually started my prayer time at the state capitol, and then proceeded to the Alabama Supreme Court building two blocks down Dexter Avenue. From there I drove to my prayer partner's home for yet another round of prayer. Personal friends often joined me in prayer at the state capitol building.

The Lord challenged me to anoint the ground and government buildings around Montgomery with anointing oil, committing them unto the Lord for righteous purposes. I purchased oil by the gallon and then poured it into smaller containers to use on the streets. I'm surprised that the Alabama State Capitol, the State House, and the Alabama Supreme Court buildings didn't slide down Dexter Avenue because they were anointed with oil so much!

I often read Scripture out loud as I prayed and walked around the capitol sidewalk on Sunday afternoons. This was my favorite Scripture that I began and ended each Sunday with: "If my people, who are called by my name, will humble themselves and pray and seek my face and turn from their wicked ways, then will I hear from heaven and will forgive their sin and will heal their land. Now my eyes will be open and my ears attentive to the prayers offered in this place" (2 Chronicles 7:14, 15).

Chapter Sixteen

UNFORGETTABLE MEMORIES

MONTGOMERY COUNTY:
JANUARY 1999 TO DECEMBER 1999

Roll Call

I was walking with my cross in Montgomery one day when I passed a very large auto-repair shop, the kind you might find at a major automobile dealership. I continued to walk for three blocks when the Lord stopped me dead in my tracks. I still remember stopping on the sidewalk and putting the cross down while I thought for a minute. I felt a powerful tug in my heart to go back to the auto-repair shop. After a time of internal wrestling, I headed back.

Before I could even reach the shop entrance, the owner came running out of his office. "Sir," he said, "I'm on the phone right now, but please walk right through my shop with your cross and make your exit at the rear door." As he was running back into his office, I gained permission to hand out gospel booklets to the mechanics as I marched through his shop. A few minutes later I exited through the back door.

The next morning I stopped by the shop again to speak with the owner. I told him I greatly appreciated the earlier opportunity. I then asked if it would be possible for me to speak to his employees at lunch one day. The owner said, "I'll do you one better than that. I'll buy my employees lunch! We'll set up tables here in the middle of the shop and eat our lunch while you talk."

A few days later I was speaking to a curious group of mechanics and office personnel. My theme was "The Shed Blood of Jesus." I talked about the sacrificial system in the Old Testament and how Jesus has now replaced that system by His blood that was shed on the cross. "Jesus forgives our sins, if we only accept Him," I stated. Then I gave an invitation, and one man, Chris, stepped forward to place his faith in Christ as I led him in the sinner's prayer.

After Chris prayed the sinner's prayer, I congratulated him on his courage to do so in front of all his peers. He replied, "I had to."

I responded, "No, you didn't have to. But you chose to and, for that, I'm so proud of you."

"Oh no, I had to," Chris retorted again. "I had to because of those dreams."

"What dreams, Chris? Please tell us about your dreams."

"Well . . . " Chris hesitated. "I've been having dreams—very scary dreams. In my dreams the Lord is calling out names, but my name is never on the roll. So you see, I had to pray that prayer!" Everyone shuddered, including myself, and some individuals started visibly shaking. I took out my New Testament and read these verses:

> "Then I saw a great white throne and him who was seated on it. Earth and sky fled from his presence, and there was no place for them. And I saw the dead, great and small, standing before the throne, and books were opened. Another book was opened, which is the book of life. . . . If anyone's name was not found written in the book of life, he was thrown into the lake of fire" (Revelation 20:11, 12, 15).

GREAT OPPORTUNITIES

So much happened in Montgomery that I can't write about it all. Here are just a few lines about some unforgettable opportunities the Lord opened:

Alabama State University

I received permission to spend the week after Easter with my cross on the campus of Alabama State University in Montgomery. ASU is comprised predominately of African-American students and is one of Montgomery's largest universities. Many eyebrows were raised those first days as I walked around campus with my 12-foot Jesus cross. I made a special effort to speak with everyone I met and to be friendly. I spoke on campus about the many convincing proofs of Christ's resurrection from the dead (Acts 1:3). Connie went with me one day and sang on the Quad between classes. One professor even allowed me to speak about Jesus Christ to her history class.

Auburn University Montgomery

I also received permission to spend a week on the campus of Auburn University Montgomery, called AUM. Two of my buddies joined me, and we had many opportunities to share Christ. I was invited to talk about Jesus to an accounting class. The following was my conclusion in class:

> "You are in this intermediate accounting class because you understand the importance of the bottom line (Net Income After Taxes) to the Profit and Loss Statement and the Balance Sheet. All of you here are 'bottom-line' people, or you would not be in this accounting class. Now, if you look at your entire life as a whole, including your birth, education, marriage and career, nothing else will determine your happiness and well-being more than being reconciled to God through our Lord Jesus Christ. That is the true bottom line of your spiritual life!"

My Apology

I often teased with students as I talked on campus. However, one girl was seemingly crushed when I teased her about a hole in her jeans (that was the style). But she walked away before I could apologize. I prayed about this matter for weeks.

One day I was in Wal-Mart 10 miles away, and I saw who I thought was this same girl working as a cashier. I stood in line and, with others listening, I apologized for offending her on campus by my teasing. She graciously accepted my apology. As I was leaving she said, "Actually, that was my sister. But I know about the incident, and I will gladly pass along your apology." I thanked the Lord for allowing me the opportunity to "eat crow" since I had obviously offended the girl.

One Disappointment

One disappointment I experienced in Montgomery was not receiving permission to minister on the campus of Huntingdon College, a school my mother graduated from in 1948.

Alabama State House

The week leading up to Palm Sunday, I ministered at the Alabama State House, which contains the chambers and offices of the Alabama state senators and representatives. I spent my time meeting with legislators one-on-one, giving them a gospel pamphlet, and praying with them for the state of Alabama. My challenge to them was this: "Think about Jesus and what He has done for us on the cross as we approach Palm Sunday and Easter." I personally knew a focus on Jesus would not be easy this week. The talk in the halls was all about the proposed lottery, which I will discuss more in the next chapter.

Montgomery Housing Projects

I spent several months walking and ministering in the poor areas of Montgomery, including a number of housing projects. Bible studies were started in some. I often drove home with tears rolling down my face while recalling the chaos I had seen that day in these rough areas.

The temptations for the residents in these places were unbelievable. While walking in one of the large housing projects one day, I noticed two ladies walking around with see-through dresses on and no underwear. I later met two men, and I had a good talk with them about Jesus. When I invited them to make a decision for Christ, they responded, "We want to know Jesus and to pray that sinner's prayer with you, but we also want sex every night with wild women!" When I told them it was one or the other, not both, they chose the wild women. The devil plays his cards, and men so easily play along, not realizing the road ahead is destruction.

An Experiment

On another occasion, I decided to try an experiment in a poor area of town to determine if I could find a man who didn't have alcohol or drugs in his bloodstream. I spent several hours on the streets that day. Most of the time it was obvious to me that people were on something (alcohol, drugs, pills) by looking into their bloodshot eyes. On occasions when I was not sure, I explained I was taking an informal survey and that I would appreciate the truth.

At the end of my walk, I had a good conversation with a man with clear eyes. I told him about my experiment, to which he responded, "I'm clean man, with nothing bad in my blood."

I exclaimed excitedly, "You're the first man I've met all day who could say that!"

"Well, actually, I did take something yesterday morning. I suppose there could still be a little bad stuff in my blood," he replied sheepishly.

I drove home emotionally crushed for the Greater Martin Luther King neighborhood, but more aware than ever of why the Lord had me on the streets.

Conversations With Spiritual Seekers

There is always fresh conversation on the streets for me to ponder. The following is a sample of conversations I had in Montgomery County with spiritually seeking individuals:

- After a long session on the streets one day, I had completely worn myself out walking and talking. I had absolutely no physical or emotional strength left in me as I walked through the Cleveland Court Housing Project on Rosa Parks Avenue. I walked up to four young men and said, "I'm too tired to talk today, but this is my question: Does anybody want to get saved?"

  They all laughed except for one man, who said, "I need to get saved!" I went through the salvation verses with this man in front of his friends, and he prayed the sinner's prayer. From this conversation sprang a Bible study that started the next week with him and his wife. They grew in the Lord over the next eight months as we met together.

- Three men made decisions for Christ one day after I found them sitting under a tree talking about the Lord. One man said, "We've been sitting here discussing things about the Lord, but we have so many questions." I was able to answer their questions and show them from Scripture how to receive forgiveness of their sins.

- While loading my cross back into my truck one afternoon, a man approached me under great conviction. He said, "I'm married and have four children, but I've been living in adultery. I saw the cross, and I'm so troubled by my situation!" We had a long conversation, after which I prayed with him for a spirit of repentance.

- A woman in ministry who had just suffered a big hurt at church was greatly comforted by seeing the cross. Thirty minutes later she drove around until she found me again, just so she could tell me that God had done a work in her heart.

- A middle-aged man named Paul stopped one day to show me a letter he carried in his billfold from his deceased mother. In the letter his mother stated, "I'm going to heaven, and I want my children to go to heaven with me." I explained to Paul how he, too, could go to heaven. Before our time was up, Paul bowed his head and asked Jesus into his heart, ensuring a reunion with his mother in heaven.

- A man stopped one day and said he had seen the cross several days earlier at a time when he had a need in his life. He said, "When I saw the cross, the Lord met my need!"

Chapter Seventeen

HOPE ABOUNDING

Statewide Lottery Referendum

On October 12, 1999, a statewide referendum was held to gain approval or disapproval of a statewide lottery. To me, its passage seemed only a formality. The big selling point for the proposed lottery was the college Hope scholarship, similar to what the state of Georgia offers. As I drove into Montgomery that morning, the Holy Spirit spoke to my heart about walking around the state capitol for several hours to pray. I was not comfortable at all with this assignment.

I wanted the message of the cross to always be about *God showing His love to us* by His shed blood. I purposely stayed away from situations where the cross could be viewed as a confusing mix of messages. I did not want people to look at the cross and think anything political. I just wanted the cross to be "Pro-Jesus,

Forgiver of our sins." But I felt a very strong tug from the Holy Spirit to head to the capitol.

Here I am walking in front of the Alabama State Capitol.

I was relieved when I arrived in front of the state capitol and everything was quiet. No promoters, protestors or crowds were present outside (although there had been plenty the day before). In fact, there was an eerie calm present.

As I walked my first lap past the front steps of the state capitol, a man stepped out of his car to speak with me. Charles, a schoolteacher from Pelham, informed me that although he was a Christian, he was very interested in seeing the lottery passed. He came to be a part of the capitol scene today for this historic vote.

I asked the schoolteacher this question, "Charles, it seems to me that our hope as individuals, and as a state, should be in Jesus alone. Why does our hope need to be in a lottery to educate our kids?"

"Paul," he responded, "I don't understand how hope in Jesus can educate anyone. How can Jesus give us dollars to be used for college?"

"Charles, we learn in Scripture to trust God for everything— our health, protection, spouse, children and job. Why can't we trust Jesus to provide funds for the education of our children too?"

"I don't know, Paul. I just have a hard time seeing Jesus as the practical answer to my children's education."

"Charles, after I walk around the capitol again, would you allow me to tell you a few stories?"

"Sure," Charles replied.

For the next six to seven hours, I alternated between walking around the state capitol in prayer and telling stories to Charles about God's provisions. After the first hour we didn't mention the proposed lottery to each other again. We talked only about Jesus and how He so graciously meets our needs. By the day's end, I had walked about 10-12 miles around the state capitol with my cross, but my mind was not on the ongoing lottery vote; Charles and I were having a spiritual revival!

The more stories I told Charles of God's provisions, the more my own spirits rose. I told Charles many stories of how God had taken care of my family these last several years as I walked with the cross. I also told Charles other stories from people we had met on the streets. The following is a sampling of the stories I told Charles that autumn day in Montgomery:

- I was walking in a very rural area of Autauga County one day, miles from a store of any kind. I was beyond thirsty; I was desperate for something to drink. But I was surrounded by nothing but forest on both sides of the road for as far as I could see. I cried out to the Lord in desperation for water. About 60 seconds later a man walked out of the forest and handed me a glass of water. What a surprise and a blessing!

  This man had just purchased a large tract of land and was walking his property to find a suitable building site. He drove his pickup truck containing a cooler into the woods. He said to me, "I was looking through the trees when, suddenly, I saw this cross coming up the road. I decided whoever was carrying that cross probably needed some water!"

- A man named John from Birmingham told me a story of a heart operation he had needed in the '70s requiring $200,000. The family did all they possibly could to raise funds, including selling a family member's home. However, they were still short by well over $100,000. John's health was declining rapidly. One night in a vision the Lord gave John names of people and phone numbers to call for help. None of these were people he knew. John made the telephone calls, and the money was raised. Three days later he flew to California, where John had a successful heart operation!

- I had been walking in Etowah County for a few weeks when I became sick with a fever and a terrible cold. On my second day of the illness, I felt compelled to get back on the streets. While I was walking it started raining, and I ended up walking six miles in the rain. I thought to myself, *This is not good. I still have a fever and a cold so bad I can't breathe. Lord, please help me!*

  When I got back to my truck, I changed into another set of clothing, which I fortunately had brought along. Driving down the road it occurred to me that I had been completely healed of both my fever and my terrible cold! I had no hint of a cold or fever from that hour on. I praised the Lord for His faithfulness.

- I met a man named Jimmy one day. Jimmy told me of an incident in which a ditch-digging machine had crushed one of his legs. He said that after the operations on his leg, he was still in a lot of pain and walked with a noticeable limp. Jimmy accepted the Lord sometime after his accident, and three months later he attended a footwashing service. As Jimmy put his shoes on after his feet were washed, it occurred to him that he had been completely healed! He started jumping up and down and praising the Lord. He could walk now without a trace of a limp.

- One day I came home riding in a wrecker with my broken-down truck in tow. Connie's vehicle was in the driveway without a working transmission. My girls were emotionally crushed. We now had no means of transportation to school or cross walk destinations, and no money was available for repairs. "What in the world are we going to do, Dad?" one daughter asked.

I did my best to calm their fears, "We've been working extremely hard and doing God's will. So now, let's sit on the front porch and pray and see how God deals with the situation." Several hours later we received an express-mail letter from my brother, Jonathan. A check was enclosed, which fully took care of our vehicle problems. I had not talked with Jonathan recently, and he knew nothing of our present difficulties.

After the stories above and many more, Charles and I ended our time with a strong Christian handshake and a prayer, in which we thanked the Lord for all His provisions. Driving home that evening, I was talking to the Lord again and recalling my experiences. I felt this day represented a positive boost in my own spiritual life. I started the morning fretting about the pending lottery referendum, which failed, but I ended the afternoon thinking only about Jesus' faithfulness.

I floated home with full victory and assurance that God would somehow help Connie and I educate our two girls for His glory! Moreover, as I recalled God's faithfulness in the past, I now felt increased *faith* and *hope* in God to meet my family's *every need* in the future! I thought about the passage from Jesus' Sermon on the Mount: "But seek first his kingdom and his righteousness, and all these things will be given to you as well" (Matthew 6:33).

Two Girls in College

As I'm finalizing this book (fall of 2006), Connie and I have sent both of our girls to college. Autumn (age 23) just graduated from Letourneau University in Texas with a bachelor's degree in flight science, a commercial pilot's license (to fly multi-engine prop airplanes), and an A&P license (airplane mechanic's license). This schooling did not come cheap! Because of the high cost of flying airplanes, Autumn's four years in college cost the equivalent of 10 full-size Chevy or Ford pickup trucks. Autumn's college expenses were paid in part by scholarships, her hard work during summers and Christmas breaks, my and Connie's contributions, and student loans. But the large remainder came from God's financial miracles.

Also, Christy (age 19), our youngest daughter, is currently attending her second year of college in Chicago. She has chosen a career in international relations and foreign languages. Her time in college is costing the equivalent of two pickup trucks per year. Once again, God is doing His mighty miracles when our resources and hard work reach their limits.

Many times during the last five years (2002-06), when our backs were absolutely against the wall with our girls' college needs, the Lord graciously heard our family's private prayers and answered them with a miracle. I am greatly humbled when I recall all the Lord has done for my two girls.

I started out this chapter telling about Charles, the schoolteacher, and the many stories I told him as evidence of God's ability to provide for our children's education. I had no way of knowing that the stories I told Charles that day in 1999 would later carry *me* through the memorable years ahead as Connie and I educated our two girls for His glory.

Chapter Eighteen

SUPREME COURT VISIT

Meeting the Justices

A s I prayed for the Alabama Supreme Court justices each week by name, the Lord began to speak to my heart about talking with them in person. I asked the Lord to open this door for me. Eventually, the Lord led me to the right people. A wonderful retired judge prayed along with me about these details. Through the retired judge's help, the Lord graciously opened an appointment for me to visit with Chief Justice Perry Hooper and several of the Alabama Supreme Court justices.

My friend, the retired judge, made sure I knew how to address the Supreme Court justices before I met with them. For example, I was instructed to refer to the chief justice with his title and not as "Mr." and surely never by his first name. The same held true with the other justices. Of course, many of you probably already know this etiquette.

I had quality one-on-one time with four of the justices. We talked about personal and spiritual matters as expected, and a few political matters. I made notes in my journal about little things I could remember about each justice.

Chief Justice Perry O. Hooper

The following is part of a conversation I had with the chief justice:

"Chief Justice Hooper, I would like to thank you for my rights of free speech and practice of religion in Alabama."

"Paul, you do realize these rights come to you by the Constitution?"

"Yes, Chief Justice, but I can't talk back to the Constitution," I explained. "However, I can thank you, since you are a representative of the highest court in Alabama."

"Oh, I understand now, Paul. You are thankful for the rights you do have, and you are exercising those rights."

"Yes, sir, I am exercising the rights of free speech and religion on the streets of Alabama, and I am eternally grateful for those rights!"

The chief justice seemed very interested and happy that I thanked him as a representative of our government for my constitutional rights.

Justice Hugh Maddox

Justice Maddox showed me the Bible he had purchased in 1945 for $7 or $8, which he earned by raising and selling chickens.

Justice Jean Brown

Justice Brown was familiar with the Bluff Park area of Hoover where I live, and we talked about this for a while. She then told me, "Please, remember to pray for us as justices." Justice Brown was surprised when I told her I drove to Montgomery every Sunday and prayed for her by name on the steps of the Alabama Supreme Court.

Justice Champ Lyons Jr.

Justice Lyons showed me a painting on his office wall of the first prayer by Congress in 1774.

This time that I spent with four of Alabama's nine Supreme Court justices helped me to personalize them in my mind and know how to better pray for them.

Help for Today

I was talking with two of the justices when one of them asked me this question: "Paul, what kind of things do you encounter on the streets?" Just days earlier I'd had an experience that was still swirling around in my heart and mind. So I shared this story with the two justices:

I was walking in a residential neighborhood in Montgomery when I noticed a group of teens gathered in the backyard of a house. A fence enclosed the yard but, since the gate was open, I walked through the gate with my cross.

I opened my mouth to speak to the teens when a man stepped from the house and started barking commands. I stepped aside as this authority figure shouted for the teens to fall into formation. The boys and girls were slowly and very reluctantly forming the three rows requested. I had no idea who these young people were, but I did know that everyone was unhappy to be there.

A teenage girl walked in late to join the others while they were still falling into formation. As the group stared at this girl, she made an obscene gesture at them with her hand. The instructor jerked his head around just in time to see this unruly display.

"Oh, that's the way you want to be today?" the instructor screamed. He began to punish the girl in a number of ways, barking out different commands to her. Because she was a bit slow to respond, he countered, "So . . . you can give it out, but let's see now if you can take it!" After that statement, he commanded the kids to form a straight line, and he placed the girl at the head of the line facing the others.

"I want you to look into the eyes of each teen here as each of them gives you that same obscene gesture. If you look away with your eyes, you must start at the head of the line again!"

Twenty boys and girls stood in that long line. The girl, perhaps 16 or 17 years old, stood in front of the first person, a boy. The boy gave her the gesture, and she looked away. He was commanded to repeat the process again while she looked into his eyes.

The girl was instructed to start the process over and over because she kept looking away. Some of the boys reluctantly gave her the gesture, but others seemed to delight in the process. She found the latter occasions very difficult and would look away, resulting in her starting over again.

Then the girl came to the first female in line and, once again, she had to start the process over. All the females appeared terribly uncomfortable taking part in this exercise.

I had been standing with my cross by my side for perhaps 20 or 30 minutes observing this whole episode. I felt crushed in my spirit for this poor girl. She obviously entered the grounds with a bad attitude, but her inner problems had now grown exponentially.

As a kid I was accustomed to the old-fashioned, strict German discipline of my father (but not of this nature), and I had survived the rigors of boot camp in the United States Marine Corps. I had also walked with my cross for four years now in many rough places of Alabama. But I had never seen humiliation like this!

No one had said a word to me since I had entered the compound, nor did I have a chance to speak. At one point the instructor walked within a few feet of me, and I asked him, "Sir, would it be possible for me to speak to these young people? Maybe I could just say a few words?"

"No, sir," the instructor barked. "This is a government program, and we can't have any religion!"

A few minutes later the ordeal finally ended. The girl was humiliated beyond description! I walked out of the gate with tears in my eyes and a heavy burden. As I glanced back, I reflected on the irony of the words on the side of the building—"Helping Hands."

The cross felt so much heavier as I walked the remaining hour back to my truck. I have two girls of my own, and I could not imagine exposing them to such an ordeal. I cried out to the Lord over and over again in prayer for this particular teen. I told the Lord I did not understand why He had put me there with those teens since I was not allowed to speak. I earnestly pleaded with the Lord for *help* for this girl.

After loading my cross into my vehicle, I headed toward home. It was mid-afternoon, and I stopped about three miles down the road for a hamburger, as was my usual routine. As I waited in line to order my burger, I was shocked to find that same girl standing in line in front of me! I couldn't believe it—here I was in a county of 200,000 people, and the Lord answered my prayer by bringing me back in contact with her!

The girl asked, "Aren't you that guy who was in the yard with a cross?"

"Yes," I replied excitedly. "But tell me, who are you? And who are the others?"

"My name is Patrice. We are all troubled teens from my high school. Some of us were caught in school with alcohol and drugs, some of us were caught with knives and guns, and some of us . . . tried to burn the school down."

"Patrice, I felt so badly for you today. I wanted so much to share two thoughts with your group today, but your instructor would not allow me. I guess the Lord has given me another opportunity."

"Yes, He has," exclaimed Patrice, with curiosity in her voice.

"This is what I wanted to say to you earlier: First, God *loves* you! With all the problems in your life, Patrice, I know you are searching for answers. I want to assure you that there is a God in heaven who greatly cares about you and who is reaching out to you with great love, not condemnation.

"The Bible says, 'For God so loved the world' (John 3:16a). Patrice, you probably feel today like you have gotten the shaft in every area of your life. But God loves you so much, and He has a wonderful plan for your life!

"Secondly, God is in the business of *helping* people! As you earnestly seek the Lord in prayer and faithfully read His Word—the Bible—the Lord will provide help to you in every area of your life. There is sufficient *help* in *Jesus* for every single day of your life. My prayer for you, Patrice, is that your life will be completely restored by the amazing grace of Jesus Christ!"

About this time the fast-food clerk asked us for our orders. A few minutes later I gave Patrice helpful literature about God to read and ample copies to share with her friends. Walking out of the restaurant, I said goodbye. Patrice smiled as she stood up straight for the first time all day.

Part 3

WHERE IS
JESUS' CROSS
TAKING YOU?

Chapter Nineteen

FACE TO FACE

My Family Now

As this book goes to print (early 2007), my family and I are happy and still growing in the Lord. My wife, Connie, continues in her dual role of helping me minister on the streets and teaching classical piano, which she loves so much. Connie, being such a sensitive creature, surrounds herself with beautiful music, beautiful flowers, and high stacks of books about beautiful things, including the Word of God.

And me . . . I'm still walking with the cross. My steps have become more measured now after walking over 8,000 miles (as of 2006) in my home state. But I also find time to teach, write, and organize special projects in many areas of Alabama. I still have a burden for the 40 counties of north and central Alabama. I've spent quality time in 25 of these 40 counties, with 15 counties still remaining to be walked. The task ahead appears absolutely daunting at times but, as I look back in time, I see God's faithfulness everywhere. I believe the same God that has been so faithful to help me in the past will also give me sufficient grace and strength for the future!

How About You?

I have told you my stories, and now I would love to hear *yours*. I welcome you to contact me at the following address:

Paul Schweigert

P.O. Box 26211

Birmingham, AL 35260-0211

Join the Philippian Jailer!

Remember the Philippian jailer in chapter 7 who was filled with so much *joy* because he had come to believe in God—he and his whole family? Maybe you, too, are ready right now to take this step of faith for yourself. If that is the case, please consider the following steps carefully.

1. *Review the salvation message.* Review the following scriptures that Danny (ch. 11) and I read so many times together before he was killed:

   - "For God so loved the world that he gave his one and only Son, that whoever believes in him shall not perish but have eternal life" (John 3:16).

   - "For all have sinned and fall short of the glory of God" (Romans 3:23).

   - "For the wages of sin is death, but the gift of God is eternal life in Christ Jesus our Lord" (Romans 6:23).

   - "For it is by grace you have been saved, through faith—and this not from yourselves, it is the gift of God—not by works, so that no one can boast" (Ephesians 2:8, 9).

- "That if you confess with your mouth, 'Jesus is Lord,' and believe in your heart that God raised him from the dead, you will be saved" (Romans 10:9).

2. *Pray the seeker's prayer.* Carefully pray the seeker's prayer (also called the sinner's prayer or the prayer of faith) that follows:

Pray the Seeker's Prayer

Dear God,
I know that I am a sinner and that
I need Your forgiveness.
Thank You for Your Son, Jesus, His death on the cross,
and His blood that paid the penalty for all my sin.
I now invite Jesus Christ to come into my heart
and life as my personal Savior.
I desire, by the power of Your Holy Spirit, to turn
away from my sins and toward You for help.
I now allow Jesus Christ to be the leader of my life.
In Jesus' name, amen.

---

3. *Decide to follow Jesus.* Sign your name on a line that follows after you have prayed the above prayer. Then date your decision as a testimony to your family and friends who will read this book after you.

I Have Decided to Follow Jesus

1. Name _____ Date _____

2. Name _____ Date _____

3. Name _____ Date _____

4. Name _____ Date _____

5. Name _____ Date _____

6. Name _____ Date _____

7. Name _____ Date _____

8. Name _____ Date _____

9. Name _____ Date _____

10. Name _____ Date _____

After Your Decision to Follow Jesus

After you have made a decision to follow Jesus, you will find the following steps helpful as you mature in your new faith. The steps below are not meant to restrict your life but to set you free from your past life of sin and bondage and into a new life of victory, purpose and hope.

Read your Bible daily. Consider starting in the Gospel of John (the fourth book in the New Testament). Read the Book of Psalms when discouraged. Read the Old Testament to learn about the lives of real people who loved God and a few who didn't. Read Proverbs to gain wisdom in dealing with people, money, work and pleasure.

Pray to God daily. Start your prayer by saying "Dear God" or "Dear heavenly Father." Then end your prayer by saying "In Jesus' name, I pray, amen." In between the opening and ending of the prayer, just talk to God the way you would a friend. Tell the Lord about your day. Tell Him you love and appreciate what He has done for you. Then explain your needs and difficult situations and ask for His help.

Find a Bible-believing church home and attend weekly. This may be the most difficult step for you, but there is no substitute for meeting with other believers. In team sports, it is impossible for you to be a great football or basketball player without being on a team. Likewise, as a Christian, you also need the give-and-take and encouragement of being involved on God's team—the church.

Be baptized in order to publicly show your identification with the Lord Jesus Christ. Water baptism is an act of obedience that symbolizes your commitment to Christ, much as a wedding ring symbolizes your commitment to your spouse.

Share your new faith with someone else. Tell your family members and friends what has happened to you. You might say, "I have recently become a Christian," or "I just got saved," or "I recently asked Christ into my heart!" Share this book with your family members and friends and ask them to join you in your new life. Like the Philippian jailer, I pray your life will be filled with great *joy* as your family comes to Christ with you.

This is a tough chapter. Actually, it is the toughest chapter in this book because it challenges you to make a commitment to Jesus. Consider if you were standing beside a road and Christ came walking by. Maybe you would say "Hello" to Him. But what if He smiled and simply replied, "Follow Me!"?

In this book I have told you hundreds of small stories as my way of sharing the gospel of Jesus Christ with you. I don't believe you have read these events by accident. In fact, I believe you are having a face-to-face encounter with Christ, not me, and He is speaking to your heart today. Jesus is saying to you what He said to those 12 men who became His disciples—"Follow Me!"

Where is Jesus' cross taking you?

What if you were standing beside a road and Christ came walking by?
What if He smiled and said, "Follow Me!"?

Chapter Twenty

A Brown Paper Bag

Walking for hours in the rain one summer day, I could feel my body getting weary from the weight of the cross. Even though my cross is made of pressure-treated pine, it absorbs considerable amounts of water—and so adds weight—when exposed to extended rainfall. So, I was struggling physically at the end of my walk in a rural area when a lady stopped her vehicle and handed me a brown paper bag.

In the paper bag I was thrilled to find a large, steaming cup of hot chocolate and a giant, warm cheeseburger. After thanking the dear saint who delivered my late lunch, I propped my cross against a fence and set the cup of hot chocolate on top of the fence post. The cup had a lid on top, so I reasoned that I would tackle that portion of my treasure later.

Because it was still pouring down rain, I knew I needed to engineer my sandwich carefully. I turned the foil down a bit and took a large bite. To protect the sandwich that remained from the rain, I turned it to a 90-degree angle and held it under the bill of my cap. In that position, I chewed my first bit of the cheeseburger. *Wow, what a delight!*

The cheeseburger was full of beef, lettuce, tomato, mustard and pickles. It all tasted so goooood! I again lowered the cheeseburger, turned the foil way down this time, and took another giant bite. Holding the bread of the remaining sandwich close to my nose, I slowly chewed another bite of the best cheeseburger in the *world*!

This time the aroma hit me full force as I enjoyed my second bite. The delicious smell was so overwhelming it brought tears to my eyes. I slowly ate the rest of the sandwich. I was in no hurry because I was enjoying the smell as much as the taste and nourishment. How in the world could something smell and taste so good?

I then picked up the cup of hot chocolate and opened the lid. To my surprise, the drink was still hot. As I drank the perfect drink for a wet, cool summer afternoon, I thought to myself, *I must have already died and gone to heaven. If not, don't wake me up now because life just doesn't get any better than this!*

How could I possibly be any happier? I'm doing what God has called me to do. I'm making countless good friends. I'm having more wonderful experiences than I ever imagined. And I have a loving wife and two precious daughters. Then, to top it all off, the Lord has given me a drive and purpose in my life every day that I never thought possible.

"Thank you, Jesus!"

And I thank *you* for reading my book.

—Your friend, Paul

NOTES

NOTES